# FOR THE

I0152945

# Display

## OF HIS

# Splendor

# Advance Praise

The needs of a hurting generation are most evident in these current days. As Amilliah notes, God is neither deaf nor blind to humanities' plight, but rather in His sovereignty, He chooses to raise up individuals through whom He works, to provide for the needs of others. We are designed with God given potential that we might display His splendor to all people. This book helps the reader step into their God-given role with confidence, through practical application with each chapter.

SUZANNE BACHELOR
Director of Spartanburg Baptist Collegiate Ministry

# FOR THE
# Display
## OF HIS
# Splendor

Stepping Out to Meet
the Needs of Our Generation

# AMILLIAH KENYA

AMBASSADOR INTERNATIONAL
GREENVILLE, SOUTH CAROLINA & BELFAST, NORTHERN IRELAND
www.ambassador-international.com

# For the Display of His Splendor

Stepping Out to Meet the Needs of Our Generation

ISBN: 978-1-64960-120-9
eISBN: 978-1-64960-170-4

Cover Design by Hannah Linder Designs
Interior Typesetting by Dentelle Design
Edited by Avrie Roberts

Scriptures taken from the King James Version of the Bible. Public Domain.

AMBASSADOR INTERNATIONAL
Emerald House
411 University Ridge, Suite B14
Greenville, SC 29601
United States
www.ambassador-international.com

AMBASSADOR BOOKS
The Mount
2 Woodstock Link
Belfast, BT6 8DD
Northern Ireland, United Kingdom
www.ambassadormedia.co.uk

*The colophon is a trademark of Ambassador, a Christian publishing company.*

*I pray for God's blessings on all who made this project a reality:*

*Pastor Davy Shelton of Gateway*

*Marjorie Earwood*

*My husband, Charles Kenya*

*My children, Daniel, Anna, Tumaini, and Kala; Hope and Harry Kenya*

# Table of Contents

PREFACE   11

FOREWORD   13

## Part One
GOD IS COUNTING ON YOU TO DISPLAY HIS SPLENDOR   15

## Chapter One
STEPPING OUT TO MEET THE NEEDS
OF OUR GENERATION   17

## Chapter Two
GOD RAISES HIS SERVANTS FOR DIFFICULT TIMES   25

## Chapter Three
ARE YOU STRAYING FROM YOUR CALLING?   33

## Chapter Four
BEWARE OF THE SCHEMES OF THE ENEMY   45

## Part Two
WHAT WILL IT TAKE TO DISPLAY GOD'S SPLENDOR?    55

### Chapter Five
WHAT WILL IT TAKE TO DISPLAY GOD'S
SPLENDOR IN OUR GENERATION?   57

### Chapter Six
DWELLING IN THE SECRET PLACE
OF THE ALMIGHTY   65

### Chapter Seven
SEEKING GOD   73

### Chapter Eight
THE TRANSFORMATION OF SPENDING
TIME WITH GOD   81

### Chapter Nine
WHAT WILL IT TAKE TO DISPLAY HIS SPLENDOR?   89

## Part Three
STEPPING OUT TO DISPLAY GOD'S SPLENDOR    101

### Chapter Ten
UNASHAMED TO DISPLAY HIS SPLENDOR   103

### Chapter Eleven
RESISTING TEMPTATION   115

### Chapter Twelve
STANDING YOUR GROUND AND ACTING   123

## Chapter Thirteen
### MAKING DELIBERATE CHOICES TO SERVE BETTER   133

## Part Four
### STEPPING OUT TO MEET THE NEEDS OF OUR GENERATION   147

## Chapter Fourteen
### PURPOSING TO ACT   149

## Chapter Fifteen
### STEP UP TO THE TIMES   161

## Chapter Sixteen
### SAY YES AND WATCH GOD WORK   171

## Chapter Seventeen
### GOD IS AT WORK IN YOUR LIFE   179

# Preface

Is your heart touched by the emotional distress, mental illness, hopelessness, despair, addiction, fear, anxiety, uncertainty, and fatigue that characterizes our days?

God is not blind to the plight of any generation. God is not deaf to the cries of His people either. However, God does not rend the heavens to descend on earth to meet the needs of each generation. He identifies vessels and works through them to bring hope and meaning. God raises men and women to meet and to combat the needs of His people in every generation.

Within the foundations of despair and hopelessness is the cry, "Can someone call on God for me?" Woven within the fabric of fear, anxiety, and deep emotional distress is a heart crying for God.

God wants you to display His splendor in this century. He is counting on you to step out and meet the needs of this generation. It is for this very reason that He created and placed you in this generation at such a time as this. You are not too insignificant for God's use. God has equipped you to meet specific needs. Won't you allow Him to guide and work through you?

# Foreword

When I think about my friends and those in the upcoming generations, a common thread is a desire to live authentically and full of purpose. All generations before have striven and continue to pursue that, but the current times uniquely apply this worldview.

We are now willing to quit high-paying successful careers if they are not aligned with our passion or feelings of morality. We are willing to sacrifice living in proximity to childhood friendships, family, comfort and security in order to explore passion for adventure, growth, and fear of complacency. We are willing to give out of our lack to help the needy. We are willing to give our lives to be used by God. In the midst of these inspiring qualities, ironically our actual lifestyle does not reflect the same level of nobility and our thoughts and philosophy towards actions are not often accompanied with longevity and peace. Despite the sacrifices, somehow, we still manage to betray our relentless desire for authenticity, purpose, and full surrender to God.

Our generation at its core can still be accurately defined by emotional restlessness, fear, and anxiety. We lack faithfulness and perseverance in what is authentic and purposeful. God knows that. He made us. Through His word, He has offered examples of successes and failures through men and women with the same desires.

This book has tangibly made that clear to me and is inspiring me to be a display of His splendor. I am encouraged, challenged, and stirred as I more clearly see how to live out the desires that my Creator has placed within me and all my friends. If you desire to explore why you habitually betray the deep desires within you, I recommend this book. Read it as you pray and seek God to clearly show you how to display His splendor. If you have a burning desire to be used by God to meet the needs that you see around you, I also recommend this book. The book leads the reader through questions, Scripture, examples, and activities to explore what is already within.

Thank you, Mama, for this book. It is changing me, and it will help future generations including your grandchildren.

DANIEL KENYA
A mentor to young people
An Engineer

# Part One

# God Is Counting on You to Display His Splendor

## Chapter One

# Stepping Out to Meet the Needs of Our Generation

*I've learned that people will forget what you said, people will forget what you did, but people will never forget how you made them feel.*

Maya Angelou[1]

### God Wants You to Display His Splendor

This century is characterized by emotional distress, mental illness, hopelessness, despair, addiction, fear, anxiety, uncertainty, and fatigue. Our generation is hurting. These present times require men and women who will step up to meet unique needs. Wherever you look, your heart is confronted with people plagued on every side. I have not seen such turmoil before. Both men and women are carrying heavy burdens. The old and the young alike are under strong emotional distress.

There seems to be a deep-rooted question in the hearts of men. This is not a question you will hear audibly. You will not see it overtly inscribed by pen on paper either. It is a question disguised well, but it surfaces prominently in

---

1    Angelou, Maya. *The Heart of a Woman*. New York: Random House, 1981.

different actions. You will be confronted with this question as you encounter acts of violence. It is the noteworthy yarn in mean, cold-hearted acts; the center of most indulgences; and the last thing that cries out in moments of despair, saying, "Can someone help me?"

God is not blind to the plight of any generation. He is not deaf to the cries of His people. However, God does not rend the heavens to descend on earth in human form as He did when He sent His Son, Jesus Christ, to redeem mankind. God uses men and women to meet the needs of each generation. He is all-powerful and He can step into the situations we face at any time and in any way, but He chooses to work with man most of the time. He identifies vessels and works through them to bring hope and meaning, using man to fulfill His purposes and to accomplish His work.

God does not play favorites, but He has favorites. Anyone can be God's favorite. Those who desire Him, those who separate themselves from the world and turn to Him, become favorite vessels for His use. Those who cleanse themselves from sin and the idols of the world become servants of noble use just as He promises in 2 Timothy 2:19-21.

"Nevertheless the foundation of God standeth sure, having this seal, The Lord knoweth them that are his. And, Let every one that nameth the name of Christ depart from iniquity.

But in a great house there are not only vessels of gold and of silver, but also of wood and of earth; and some to honour, and some to dishonour.

If a man therefore purge himself from these, he shall be a vessel unto honour, sanctified, and meet for the master's use, and prepared unto every good work."

Those who get to the inner courts with God experience Him. Those who tarry and lean on His bosom, touching His heart like the Apostle John, hear Him. They feel His heartbeat for the world, and bear His burden for their generations. They see what many do not as they behold the eyes of their Master. Their ears fill up with God's message to His people. As they arise from His presence, they have tidings of hope and grace for the troubled hearts of men. It is no wonder that it was John, the man beloved by God, who leaned on the Savior's chest, who received the revelations of God. He saw and witnessed the mysteries of God while on the island of Patmos to the edification of the church.

God raises men and women to meet and to combat the needs of His people in every generation. Those who are willing to follow God take part in His mission. Those who are willing to believe and trust Him become God's vessels for their times. They witness His hand at work through them and by them. They display His splendor.

As evidenced in 2 Timothy 2:19-21, every Christian is a candidate for God's noble use. As long as your heart walks away from sin and purposes to follow Him, you will be a vessel for use.

Within the foundations of despair and hopelessness is the cry, "Can someone call on God for me?" Woven within the fabric of fear, anxiety, and deep emotional distress is a heart crying for God. Those fearful, bewildered, and distressed do not know how to reach Him.

A distressed man cannot worship. A fearful and dismayed woman cannot see God. Emotional despair is a thick, dark blanket on the soul of man. It is a tool of the enemy that blinds man's sight and overshadows God.

God will work with men and women who will seek Him for the sake of this generation. God is waiting for those who will hear the deep cries of this age, those whose hearts will stir up with a desire for action and a solution. God will work with anyone who will go past the pleasures and the correctness of our days. Those who will overlook the favor and applause of men will crack through the façade of our times to meet deep-rooted needs.

*Will you display God's splendor?*

When the children of Israel faced hard labor and bondage in their land of captivity, God sent Moses to Egypt. He used a mere human being, a simple man, to do what was humanly impossible. The world witnessed with shock and astonishment as God worked amongst millions of people journeying through the wilderness. His people were delivered. They threw away their chains and walked in newness of life to worship and serve their God. Many people in our generation are in bondage, and their chains neither give them freedom nor a chance to see and worship God.

You are God's candidate for our times.

## God Raises People for Special Times

Israel settled in the land of Canaan just as God promised. He set kings, prophets, and priests to govern over His people, and He gave His people rest. "And it came to pass, when the king sat in his house, and the Lord had given him rest round about from all his enemies; That the king said unto Nathan the prophet, See now, I dwell in an house of cedar, but the ark of God dwelleth within curtains. And Nathan said to the king, Go, do all that is in thine heart; for the Lord is with thee" (2 Samuel 7:1-3).

David desired to make God the central theme of Israel. He knew that it was as long as God indwelled and lived among His people that the children of Israel would remain blessed and fulfilled. He set his heart to build a house for the ark of the Lord. It would be a place of worship, where man communed with God for the healing of the soul, mind, and body.

However, God did not choose David to build the house of worship for Israel. He chose Solomon, David's son. Take a moment to reflect on God's choice for the special task. Look at the man chosen to build a magnificent place where millions would gather for worship. It was not Jesse, the father of the king. It was not Nathan, the prophet to the king either. It was Solomon, born to David and Bathsheba.

It is easy to disqualify yourself from God's candidates, but remember that God chooses and uses the unlikeliest of people. He, Who formed you, also knows how He wired you. He knows the treasures He wove into your fibers for His work and for the display of His splendor. Yes, God can disqualify a man from His work. Nevertheless; He works with fallible men and women. That is all He has. Don't disqualify yourself, but rather align yourself with God. Seek Him. Follow closely and listen with keenness. God does not cast away anyone who comes to Him. So, regardless of the circumstances that surrounded you when you came to this world, you are a candidate.

## God Raises People for Special, Hard Tasks

The issues that fill our generation are not easy, and will be solved only by daring people willing to take a stand while aligning with God. It will take men and women of integrity who will speak the truth of God in love. It will take those whose hearts beat with a true and honest desire to see the hearts of people healed and turned back to God. Those entangled in the business of filthy lucre at the expense of the souls of men will only increase the pain of our times.

God chooses people for such tasks in this generation. He is stirring their hearts into action and making them restless every day as He points them to others' agony. He equips and makes provisions for His work.

There was another time when God's chosen people faced tough days because of sin. The city where the magnificent temple was built by King Solomon was destroyed. Its walls were broken and the gates burned down. The place of worship was reduced to ruins. God's people were taken captive and exiled. The temple that once rang with the praises of God was abandoned. God's sanctuary that once filled with the glory and presence of God became a territory and a strong hold for the enemies of God. God's people who once rejoiced in the hallowed place where they met with Him were scattered. The peace they once enjoyed turned into fear, dismay, and hopelessness. The courage that made them walk tall with confidence was reduced to uncertainty, panic, and despair.

God's people lost His touch and presence, forfeiting His power. No longer could they stand against their enemies. They found out that without the nearness of their Heavenly Father, they were as frail as dust, and had no power of their own to oust their enemies. They found themselves running from the enemy who was in constant pursuit as their backs were pressed against the wall. They were under the dictum of the enemy, and life was miserable. It was while under the chains of the enemy and no longer enjoying the freedom of their own land that they understood God's favor. True joy and peace prevail when God is in His rightful place. Soundness of mind, body, and soul are enjoyed as God inhabits His central place. Goodness, fulfillment, fruitfulness, and even prosperity are by-products of God's presence, love, and mercy.

God does not leave His children in endless despair and helplessness. He chose a militant man serving under an ironhanded ruler. God stirred the heart of Nehemiah the prophet, the cupbearer to the Persian Emperor, Artaxerxes (Nehemiah 1-2).

Sometimes, it is not easy to know how gifted you are until God thrusts you into tough situations. Nehemiah was God's example for this. He set about rebuilding the walls and gates of Jerusalem. This chosen servant burned with the desire to restore the hearts of people back to their all-sufficient God. The few Jews who escaped captivity and remained in Jerusalem had only one hope—God. He alone could take away their shame and humiliation and restore their respect and dignity.

Even though Nehemiah was backed up by the king he served, little did he know the opposition and warfare that awaited him. Sanballat and Tobiah were indignant and mocked the Jews. Sanballat drafted men into the army of Samaria to oppose Nehemiah and his work crew (Nehemiah 4).

Little did Sanballat and Tobiah know that Nehemiah was a representative of the Most High God who had been raised for that tough time. God had a leader, a planner, and an executor, one who would rally a troop to work. He was militant and daring, and stood in the face of threats. His job in the palace of Shushan had been good training ground for the work God had for him.

Tough times demand strong, godly leadership. God has many gifted leaders and many of His children in well-selected areas today. Knowingly or unknowingly, they are trained to effectively meet the spiritual needs of this generation. There is a fierceness, a boldness, and a holy fire in the hearts of men and women called to this work. Do not hesitate to step out to meet the needs of our times. Gather your troops. Seek God and let Him lead and work through you to pursue the spiritual, emotional, and physical welfare of others.

## Activities to Help You Display the Splendor of God

This century is characterized by emotional distress, mental illness, hopelessness, despair, addiction, fear, anxiety, uncertainty, and fatigue. Within the foundations of despair and hopelessness is the cry, "Can someone help me? Can someone call on God for me?"

1.   What does God seem to be saying to you? For what cause is He stirring your heart? Write it down.

2.   Identify people who can benefit from your help. These may be your neighbors, co-workers, friends, relatives, church, or organizations you know.

3.   In what practical ways can you help? Whom should you approach for help?

4.   Step up and do it.

## Memory Verses

*Then shall the King say unto them on his right hand, Come, ye blessed of my Father, inherit the kingdom prepared for you from the foundation of the world:*

*For I was an hungred, and ye gave me meat: I was thirsty, and ye gave me drink: I was a stranger, and ye took me in:*

*Naked, and ye clothed me: I was sick, and ye visited me: I was in prison, and ye came unto me.*

Matthew 25:34-36

## Chapter Two

# God Raises His Servants for Difficult Times

*I learned that courage was not the absence of fear, but the triumph over it . . .*
*The brave man is not he who does not feel afraid, but he who conquers that fear.*

Nelson Mandela[2]

## You Are God's Choice for These Times

When people forsake God, certain characteristics become evident.

When man breaks God's holy laws, the initial reaction is to run away and hide. A heart that is running and hiding is anxious. It knows what is right from what is wrong, fearing that God Who sees and knows all things is aware of what is happening. Such a heart does not know whether to expect a reprimand or a pardon. This heart cannot pray to the God from whom it is running, nor stay still to read God's Word because it is afraid of what God will say. This heart's greatest need is restoration and reassurance of the Father's love and forgiveness. This is where we all find ourselves in our moments of wandering and straying from God.

---

2    Mandela, Nelson. *Long Walk to Freedom: The Autobiography of Nelson Mandela.* United Kingdom: Little, Brown & Company, 1994.

A heart that is left unrestored is faced with two choices.

The first choice is to keep running and hiding. This heart goes underground and remains in hiding. It fights shame and fear. It slowly withdraws from prominent places of service and worship. It lurks behind and follows others at a comfortable distance and avoids situations where the cause of their running and hiding may be confronted. It will settle down to be a passive observer.

This heart is unaware that it has stepped into a more difficult territory. The claws of Satan await it. The enemy ridicules and scorns it. He rails accusations and plagues its conscience. This heart drifts into defeat, hopelessness, and despair. Such individuals may easily drop from the company of God's people. Some beat themselves to death mentally as they work out their restitution through various good works. They may tithe more, give money to humanitarian causes, and go out of their way to help others as they try to appease God. All the while, their hearts cry, "Can someone help me?"

The second choice for the unrestored heart is to seek solace from the same cistern which yielded momentary pleasure. The heart of man is created with a deep-rooted desire for God and for worship. When these spiritual pangs gnaw within us, our hearts embark on a search. Unfortunately, when one is unaware of how to gratify the spiritual need, he wanders between different earthly pacifiers, temporarily placated by pleasure and entertainment. In reality, the real need is silenced, and its intensity calmed by the circumstantial happenings one surrounds themselves with.

A heart that is seeking a thrill is an easy target for the enemy. Satan is a mastermind at such games. The adversary works to lure hearts into sin and to hold them captive—constantly seeking and going back to that exhilarating rush of energy. As is evident in our generation, nothing wearies the heart of man and leaves him empty like sin and pleasure.

Sin and pleasure leave us sick, empty, and hopeless. Since the delights of wrongdoing are mere pacifiers, they do not satisfy, but rather lead to disappointment and enslavement. With no seeming solution, man returns to what only increases hopelessness. This is how many people find themselves enslaved by strange indulgences and addictions from which they cannot break free. In vain, they plunge deeper in hopes of finding satisfaction, joy, and peace.

Remember, the pleasure-seeking heart needs restoration. Failing to reinstitute such an individual results in deep disappointment, which can easily turn into anger. When left unattended, anger surfaces in acts of rebellion, showing its prominent streaks through violence and an increase of crimes. Coldness, indifference, and heartlessness become the common traits that characterize society—the societies in which we live, I am afraid, being well depicted here.

## God Raised Gideon to Help God's People at a Difficult Time

Difficult times require strong, godly leadership. Days of lawlessness demand a countering voice of God. Such a voice comes through unswerving men and women of faith. They correctly diagnose the spiritual maladies of the times and guide people to the healing balm. They do it diligently, boldly, tenderly, and without compromise, and understand the only thing that cures spiritual gangrene. It is the atoning precious blood of the Lamb, the only Son of God. They understand what sustains man and keeps him fulfilled and at peace. It is the resurrecting power of the Lord Jesus Christ indwelling and working in the life of the believer.

God raised Gideon to help His people at another difficult time in Israel's history. God delivered them into the hands of the Midianites because of their sin. The Midianites prevailed so strongly against God's people that the children of Israel were forced to live in mountains, caves, and strongholds. The sin that once gave them pleasure resulted in them abandoning the safety of their homes to seek refuge in hiding.

The Midianites joined forces with the Amalekites and other Eastern nations to frustrate Israel. "And they encamped against them, and destroyed the increase of the earth, till thou come unto Gaza, and left no sustenance for Israel, neither sheep, nor ox, nor ass.

For they came up with their cattle and their tents, and they came as grasshoppers for multitude; for both they and their camels were without number: and they entered into the land to destroy it.

And Israel was greatly impoverished because of the Midianites; and the children of Israel cried unto the Lord" (Judges 6:4-6).

God's people were reduced to vagabonds and paupers in their own land. They lived in constant fear and uncertainty, never knowing when or how they would be attacked. Their labors did not satisfy either.

In their fear and distress, the children of Israel cried out to God for help. There is our question again, surfacing from a rebellious heart that is oppressed: "Can someone help me?"

> God pointed His people to the cause of their plight, saying, "I brought you up from Egypt, and brought you forth out of the house of bondage;
>
> And I delivered you out of the hand of the Egyptians, and out of the hand of all that oppressed you, and drave them out from before you, and gave you their land;
>
> And I said unto you, I am the LORD your God; fear not the gods of the Amorites, in whose land ye dwell: but ye have not obeyed my voice" (Judges 6:8-10).

He chose Gideon to deal with the enemies of Israel and to help His people. Gideon, like the rest of the Israelites, was fearful. Just like you and me, he did not know how God could use a simple man for such a big task. God sent an angel who found Gideon threshing his wheat in Ophrah while hiding from the Midianites by the winepress.

Look at what Gideon thought of himself, as opposed to what God knew about him, as recorded in the salutation of the angel whom God sent to Gideon:

"And the angel of the Lord appeared unto him, and said unto him, The Lord is with thee, thou mighty man of valour.

And Gideon said unto him, Oh my Lord, if the LORD be with us, why then is all this befallen us? and where be all his miracles which our fathers told us of, saying, Did not the LORD bring us up from Egypt? but now the LORD hath forsaken us, and delivered us into the hands of the Midianites" (Judges 6:12-13).

What man of valor was God talking about? The one hiding from the enemy? The fearful and shaking man? One who had lost faith in God and His power to deliver?

The Lord charged Gideon and encouraged him. "And the LORD looked upon him, and said, Go in this thy might, and thou shalt save Israel from the hand of the Midianites: have not I sent thee?" (Judges 6:14). Still, Gideon did not believe that God would do as He said. After all, how could the Almighty God work with a man who could not amount to anything? He was poor and the unlikeliest of men in his family to accomplish anything worthwhile.

That did not stop God. Those who display God's splendor also belong to His list of the unlikeliest candidates and misfits. God, Who trains and molds people for their times, knew Gideon very well. He proceeded to encourage the fearful man saying, " . . . Surely I will be with thee, and thou shalt smite the Midianites as one man" (Judges 6:16).

Gideon still needed assurance. He proceeded to ask for signs to build and cement his confidence with God. The Lord was patient and did as Gideon asked.

Gideon did not know that he was an answer to the question of men's hearts! "Can someone help me?" He was God's chosen vessel to display His splendor in response to the cries of the people. In his own eyes, he was a wimp, a grasshopper, a nobody. To God, and to the enemies of God's people, he was a mighty vessel. A man of valor. In his own eyes, he had neither potential nor a chance to fight against the Midianites and the Amalekites. But to God, he was a chosen man and well equipped to subdue His enemies.

God does not make mistakes. When He chooses you to do His work, you can be sure of results. Regardless of what you think of yourself or how you view yourself, God's touch and power transform and equip you for the task, however difficult.

God asked Gideon to tear down the altar of Baal erected by his father and to cut down the wooden images. God wanted an altar built for Him instead. The cause of the people's turmoil was idolatry. They didn't know that most of their pain was self-inflicted. God's heart ached for them. He longed to heal them.

In his fear, Gideon must have wrestled with endless questions. In a situation that mirrors the days in which we live, his questions could echo through the centuries to our own day: "Why me? Who can stand against the current practices of our day and survive? Who can withstand the opposition of the people? Will anyone listen? Do they care?"

Gideon feared the people so he did exactly what many of us would do. He did it at night because he feared his father's household and the men of the city (Judges 6:25).

God did not let go of Gideon. As God usually does when He calls someone to His work, Gideon's heart remained restless. There was no doubt that he was God's chosen vessel to the oppressed men and women of the land.

The Midianites and the Amalekites gathered in the Valley of Jezreel to wage war against Gideon and the people of God. The Spirit of the Lord came upon Gideon, and the coward quickly turned into the warrior. Gideon blew the trumpet and assembled troops for battle (Judges 6:33-34). Slowly, Gideon embraced his assignment. God had shaped a man for his time and molded a servant to display His glory and splendor.

God sized down Gideon's vast army to three hundred men. This was a good reminder that it was not for them to claim glory but to display the splendor, the power, and the majesty of God (Judges 7:2-3).

## With God, Victory Is Sure

When God chooses and sends His men and women to accomplish a task, victory is sure. Why would He send you in the first place if He did not desire to help His people? The battle is already won by God. You go only to manifest His victory, power, and might.

That is exactly what God did with Gideon when He said, " . . . Arise, go down . . . I have delivered it into your hand . . . " (Judges 7:9).

The battle was won before Gideon stepped onto the battleground. Even their enemies knew they were dead men under the sword of the Lord and of Gideon. Their hearts melted with so much fear that they dreamt about their defeat, and confessed that God had delivered the Midianites and the entire camp into the hand of Gideon (Judges 7:13-14). They had no courage to resist Gideon and his men.

The enemy digs deep and claims territory as long as no one is fighting and challenging him. He howls threats and intimidates as long as no one is daring enough to trust God and fight. It is no wonder God reminds us to resist the enemy. "Submit yourselves therefore to God. Resist the devil, and he will flee from you" (James 4:7). Our adversary cannot withstand fierce Christians charging at him as they trust and follow God.

Gideon did not go against the vast army with drawn swords as he had feared and anticipated. God had already won the victory, as He promised. God asked Gideon to give a trumpet and an empty pitcher with torches inside to each man. At Gideon's command, all the men blew the trumpets, broke the pitchers, and shouted, "The sword of the LORD, and of Gideon" (Judges 7:16-20).

The results were astounding. The Midianites and the Amalekites fled as God set every man's sword against his companion throughout the whole camp. The enemies fought against themselves (Judges 7:21-24). They did not lift their hand against Israel anymore, and the country was quiet for forty years in the days of Gideon (Judges 8:28).

Many in our own time are under heavy oppression of the enemy. Many maladies we see today point to the overwhelming enslavement by the adversary.

Oppressed and enslaved people are chained by the enemy. They cannot fight to set themselves free. They are crying for deliverance. Someone must step out to fight for their spiritual freedom.

Who will step out to combat the spiritual challenges of our times? Who will step out to display God's splendor? Who will go against the tides of our day? The fearful and the cowardly will not help the people. Who will obey God for the sake of the people? Is God tugging at your heart to act? Is your heart stirred for this noble task? God still sets the captives free.

## Activities to Help You Meet the Needs of Our Generation

Crushed and repressed people are enslaved by the enemy. They cannot fight to set themselves free regardless of how much they cry for deliverance and freedom. Someone must step out to fight for them.

1.  Do you know people who are oppressed and chained by the enemy? Who are they? Write down their names.

2.  What can you do to help them? Whom should you contact for help? Identify people with whom to share your burden.

3.  In what ways can your family get involved?

4.  What can your church do to help?

5.  Take a step of faith as you pray and do what you can to help the people you have identified.

## Memory Verses

*The Spirit of the Lord GOD is upon me; because the LORD hath anointed*
*me to preach good tidings unto the meek; he hath sent me to bind up the*
*brokenhearted, to proclaim liberty to the captives, and the opening of the*
*prison to them that are bound; To proclaim the acceptable year of the LORD,*
*and the day of vengeance of our God; to comfort all that mourn.*

Isaiah 61:1-2

# Chapter Three

# Are You Straying from Your Calling?

*People, even more than things, have to be restored, renewed, revived, reclaimed, and redeemed. Never throw out anyone.*

Audrey Hepburn[3]

## You Are Called by God to Display His Splendor

God does not let an entire community, let alone a whole nation, stray from Him without appointing able servants to restore them back to God. It is not God's desire that any should perish but that all should come to repentance (2 Peter 3:9).

God created you with this generation in mind. God formed you with this nation in mind, too. God designed men and women with special abilities, specific qualities, and potential, allowing them to be born in this century. That is because He had the needs of His people in mind. He is sovereign. Nothing occurs to Him. The chains of oppression that prevail in our day do not take Him by surprise. He knows us inside and out and does not depend on anyone's testimony about the men and women He created. He knew what

---

3    Hepburn, Audrey. Hellstern, Melissa. *How to be Lovely: The Audrey Hepburn Way of Life.* United Kingdom: Dutton, 2004.

would characterize individuals, families, communities, and nations at such a time in the history of mankind. He has vessels prepared to meet the needs of our times.

There are many who are reading this content as the Spirit of God bears witness that they are called to such a cause. There are those whose hearts are burning to do God's work.

Where there is a call from God for specific tasks, you will find two groups of servants. I am referring to those appointed and raised by God for that specific work.

You will find a group immersed in the work of their calling. They believe God and step out and pursue His call. Faithfully, they will stay with the tasks as God enables and opens doors. Such individuals find new avenues for ministering to the spiritual, emotional, mental, and physical needs of the people. They rally troops, plan, and strategize. They are intentional and deliberate about their calling. God responds and enables them to display His splendor in marvelous and powerful ways. He blesses the work of their hands and opens more doors as He enables them to meet the needs of the generation.

Nevertheless, you will not miss the second group of men and women, who have strayed from their calling. Their walk, with regard to their purpose, can be found inscribed in the words of the Apostle John in 1 John 2:15-17:

> "Love not the world, neither the things that are in the world. If any man love the world, the love of the Father is not in him.
>
> For all that is in the world, the lust of the flesh, and the lust of the eyes, and the pride of life, is not of the Father, but is of the world.
>
> And the world passeth away, and the lust thereof: but he that doeth the will of God abideth for ever."

The second group subdivides itself into three categories.

## Category One

The first category includes people who strayed from their calling because of a lucrative career. It has gifted men and women with a clear call from God on their lives, having been anointed by God for His work. They are talented and equipped to effectively serve God in this generation, many of whom have followed God wholeheartedly at some point. They have seen and witnessed the power and the majestic working of God. They know exactly what it will take to meet the needs of our time, yet they remain merely aware of God's calling on their lives.

These individuals know what it means to seek God. They know what it means to have the favor of God in their lives. In fact, in the course of seeking Him, while working jobs and pursuing financial stability for themselves and their families, they found themselves at a crossroads. God favored them and blessed their labors, allowing them to prosper. God established them. It was at this point that straying from their call started. They liked what they saw. They even blessed God for their success and prosperity.

However, they did not stop at that. They devoted more time toward their success. They planned and set up good objectives toward their advancement. They invested and put plans and people in place to foster growth. Slowly, their career advancement and financial success took prominence. Their focus on the work of God weakened over time. The course for which God called them started losing intensity. Their hearts developed a level of indifference. You will find a cynical and critical tone in their motives. They may support people who pursued calls that are similar to theirs. They may even seek opportunities to minister to people in their area of calling.

Straying from your call because of a lucrative career is not always intentional. Most people do not realize how good things make them drift away from a definite call. God hears and answers prayer. When you seek Him, you can be sure to find Him. When you call, He will answer. He honors His Word. He blesses the work of our hands. Those who seek Him lack no good thing. As you seek Him, He blesses you with numerous blessings in different spheres of your life. You must guard against the lure of Satan to deviate you from God's course. You must remain sober in the midst of success to hear and follow God. You must devote more time, energy, and resources to what matters most. Do not stray from your call.

## Category Two

The second category has those who strayed from their call because of compromise. Most people in this group stepped out to do the work to which God called them. However, they strayed with time and they can no longer meet the needs of this generation. Compromise, like the lucre of a prominent and successful career, creeps up on you unannounced.

Compromise loses ground when one desires the favor of the people. Ministry can be tough. Depending on the needs to which someone is called, they may face opposition from the beginning. Not many people remain relentless in their work when faced with constant opposition. When the course is steep and tough to climb, the heart yields to the desire to be liked. It craves the support of other people. It is in seeking favor and desiring to keep people's support that we shift our focus from God and His calling for our lives. Every time we step out to do the work, we are overly cautious in how we present it. The response of other people becomes a major issue of concern.

Category two is filled with servants of God who struggle with the desire to belong and to be accepted. It has anointed men and women who fear resentment, and many whose hearts run away from ridicule and criticism from opposing groups.

God's work can isolate people. Sometimes it calls for being a lonely voice without the support of others. This is not a comfortable place to live. It is hard to maintain your course when God seemingly does not show up every day to support and to encourage you. It is easy to get cold when your eyes cannot see the evidence of His presence or working.

God's servants in this category are plagued with guilt as they observe world trends and see many people languishing in spiritual, emotional, and mental apathy. In their embarrassment and shame, they understand their calling. However, many do not know how to break free in order to carry out God's mission.

## Category Three

Category three has God's anointed servants who strayed from their call because of untamed passions. Many of these servants started well and stepped into thriving and promising works for God. They obeyed God and stepped into their call with zeal and vigor. They tasted and witnessed God's touch and power. They know how to minister to the needs of our generation. They are gifted and talented by God for the work. They are wise, smart, and knowledgeable, created and selected for our time. God has put them in opportune places and given them the right network of people to do His work.

Unfortunately, these men and women have lost the anointing and the touch of God. They have fallen from God's place of service because they could not tame their passions.

### Understanding the Power of Untamed Passions

What will it take to display God's splendor in your days? Conversely, what can stop you from displaying His splendor? One thing that will rob you of God's power and the ability to display His splendor is an untamed passion.

Samson, a great man of God, gives us a true glimpse of the struggles that characterize God's servants in this category.

Samson, like many of God's chosen servants today, was born to accomplish specific work for God. He was born at a time when God's people were under the heavy oppression of the Philistines. Samson was born to deliver the children of Israel from the overwhelming and overpowering hand of their enemy, who had subdued them for forty long years.

God created His servant, Samson, in response to the cries and the afflictions of His people. Judges 13 opens with God delivering His beloved children into the hands of the Philistines because of their sin. However, within the same breath, He also points us to a barren couple. At a time of great distress and trouble in the land, God decided to give that couple a child to deal with the reproach on His people. You cannot help but think of the truth of God's holy Word in Ephesians 2:10: "For we are his workmanship, created in Christ Jesus unto good works, which God hath before ordained that we should walk in them."

God does not create for the sake of creating or populating the world. Every individual is created to fulfill and to accomplish very specific purposes. He responds to the needs of the world by creating specific people to meet them at very specified times. You are one of them.

Being set apart for God's purposes demands living up to certain standards set by God. He also holds certain families to stipulated requirements and standards if they are to rise and accomplish His work. This was the case for Manoah and his wife. Their instructions from God were clear: "Drink not wine nor strong drink, and eat not any unclean thing . . . thou shalt conceive, and bear a son; and no razor shall come on his head: for the child shall be a Nazarite unto God from the womb: and he shall begin to deliver Israel out of the hand of the Philistines" (Judges 13:4-5).

The child chosen to end the fear, distress, shame, and hopelessness among God's people would be a Nazarite from birth until his death.

A Nazarite? Who is a Nazarite?

Nazarite is derived from the Hebrew word *nazir*. It refers to an individual consecrated and set apart to the service of God. It is an office or position of separating yourself in holiness unto God for His work and purposes.

Nazarites, according to Numbers 6:1-21, observed three statutes: (1) they abstained from wine and strong drink, (2) they did not cut their hair, and (3) they did not come in contact with the dead.

In reality, there was more to the vow than restricting drinks, maintaining one's hair, and not attending funerals. It was a calling. The greater importance lay in the reasons behind the abstinence and restrictions.

Those who will be fully used in God's timely missions must cautiously watch for what defiles and diminishes their effectiveness. They must understand what desecrates them. They must comprehend what stops God from working through them.

Our indulgences, preoccupations, and participations dictate the extent to which we serve God. These can be inferred from the Nazarite vows.

Samson fell short of his calling. Instead of separating himself in holiness to be a vessel "meet for the Master's use," he indulged in what dishonored his service and was obsessed with pleasure. His untamed passions of self-gratification loomed high until they marred his calling and mission. He overstepped his God-given boundaries until he found himself bound and chained by the very bonds he was born to break and destroy. Samson sought and followed seductive pleasure from the camps of God's enemies.

Samson's first step toward straying from the call of God started as a normal human desire. At a certain stage in life men look for women. Women do the same. However, look at Samson's path. "And Samson went down to Timnath, and saw a woman in Timnath of the daughters of the Philistines . . . And he went down, and talked with the woman; and she pleased Samson well" (Judges 14:1, 7).

Samson sought intimate relationships in the camps of his enemy. Philistia was not the place for a child of God to play with and kindle the fires of untamed passions. Those were fierce enemies of the Lord's people. Samson paid a costly price for taking that woman as his wife. Had it not been for the Spirit of God, Samson would have paid with his life.

Samson's passions escalated. He went to Gaza, saw a harlot, and consorted with her (Judges 16:1). Gaza was one of the major Philistine cities. Samson was back in the enemy's territory. The Philistines seemed to understand the reason for Samson's birth more than Samson himself. When they heard that Samson was in town, they surrounded the place and lay in wait for him all night hoping to kill him (Judges 16:2). God still used those incidents to accomplish the mission for which He created His servant.

After such deadly encounters, one would assume that learned lessons would lead to restraint. Not for Samson.

## Let Us Apply It

Like Samson, untamed passions can blind people from the mission for which they were created. Impetuous passions degrade and reduce men and women of integrity into paupers and slaves. They strip them of their dignity and push them into filthy trenches. God's men and women find themselves in dismay as they look at the sinful pleasures that drew them from reputable positions and prestigious works of service. As they look back to the first step that led to their captivity, they writhe in pain and shame. Like Samson, they discover that it is a trap that leads only to deeper and deeper entanglement. Even more painful is the realization of how hard it is to break free of those traps.

Sometime later, Samson fell in love with a woman in the Valley of Sorek named Delilah (Judges 16:4). This time, Samson did not know that the rulers of the Philistines had a secret plan to lure and to exterminate God's man from accomplishing his work.

Do not underestimate the power behind what is luring you from God and your mission in this world. Passions gnaw at our hearts relentlessly. They can blind our spiritual perception and alter our physiology as they infest our bones with an unholy fire that is difficult to extinguish. They lead us from a path of reality and fill us with unrealistic assumptions, keeping us in a land of fake dreams.

Samson, God's anointed servant, could not perceive the dreadful schemes of the enemy. While in full pursuit of gratification, the enemy subdued him right there in the very cistern of his momentary delight. The Philistines bound Samson while his head was in Delilah's lap.

Look at the subtle lure that took place before the Philistines captured Samson. The Philistines set up a strategic plan for apprehending an enemy that is still effective even in our world today. They were intentional in their purpose. Let us look at this planned scheme.

## 1. Identify the enemy.

You target those who trouble the kingdom of Satan and evaluate their effectiveness and where their influence is highest. You diligently study their modes of operation.

The enemy identified the man chosen and anointed to fight against them.

Beware, Satan, the enemy of your soul, is always on this mission. Men and women who set their hearts to seek, hear, follow, obey, and serve God wholeheartedly are surveyed and schemed upon constantly.

## 2. Come up with ways of capturing and conquering the enemy.

You access your potential in relation to that of the enemy. You weigh your power against the enemy's abilities and capabilities.

The Philistines acknowledged their vulnerabilities and inabilities against the man. God's enemies understood that anointed servants of the Most High God are strong and powerful. They have divine spiritual strength and power. You cannot bring them down without a good master plan, and that is what the enemies of God did. They set their hearts and minds to find and subdue the power in Samson's life.

## 3. Use cleverly selected baits and schemes to lure the enemy until you seize him.

One effective method is to play with the weaknesses of your enemy.

As you conspire on his strengths and weaknesses, you devise and craft baits that appeal to his appetites. You offer him what he cannot resist easily. You give what ignites his passions. All the while, you remain intentional with your goal.

For Samson, it was women.

### 4. Disguise your baits in order to crack and unravel the enemy one layer at a time.

You work your way to the deep secrets as you move closer to your objective.

That is how Delilah executed her plans with skill and expertise as she rocked the man of God who helplessly lay in her lap on the greatest day of his regret.

The first was a disguised casual inquiry. "Tell me, I pray thee, wherein thy great strength lieth, and wherewith thou mightest be bound to afflict thee," she asked. It sounds normal for a good friend to be impressed with your seeming supernatural strength. There is nothing alarming at knowing the source of such strength. However, the last portion of that request should have sounded a subtle alarm in Samson's mind. What was her intention in saying . . . "wherewith thou mightest be bound to afflict thee?"

This must confirm the words of Jesus in Matthew 12:34b, "for out of the abundance of the heart the mouth speaketh." That statement revealed the motive behind her investigation. Nevertheless, Samson either ignored or missed the caution. A reasonable response, before fooling Delilah, could have been a counter question desiring to know why she wanted to bind him.

### Activities to Help You Remain Steadfast in Your Calling

God created you with this generation in mind. God formed you with this nation in mind, too. God has equipped you with enough resources and tools to help you stand in this generation. God has not left you to fate.

1.   Do you have untamed passions? What are they?

2.   What baits is the enemy using to draw you from God and from His service?

3.   In what ways is he using your passions to frustrate or hinder the work of God in your life?

4.   Begin to note how many times you fall or succumb to your passions in a day. Take note of what precedes each occurrence and the impact it has on you afterwards.

5.   Make that passion a matter of specific prayer. Be honest with God about it. Ask Him to give you victory. Start working on ways to overcome it.

## Memory Verses

*Blessed is the man that endureth temptation: for when he is tried, he shall receive the crown of life, which the Lord hath promised to them that love him.*

*Let no man say when he is tempted, I am tempted of God: for God cannot be tempted with evil, neither tempteth he any man:*

*But every man is tempted, when he is drawn away of his own lust, and enticed.*

*Then when lust hath conceived, it bringeth forth sin: and sin, when it is finished, bringeth forth death.*

James 1:12-15

*Chapter Four*

# Beware of the Schemes
# of the Enemy

*All of God's people are ordinary people who have been made extraordinary
by the purpose he has given them.*

Oswald Chambers[4]

The motive of the enemy for the man or woman who desires to walk in obedience to their calling remains the same to date. Satan comes to kill, to steal, and to destroy (John 10:10).

Behind every lure and deceptive scheme of the enemy is the desire to take away your spiritual influence. Look beyond worldly pleasures, regardless of their gratification. There is no free pleasure from the enemy of God. Satan is working to break you and defeat you. He will leave you empty, powerless, and marred for God's service. Beware, his ultimate scheme is to destroy you.

The enemy is always on a deadly mission with his adversary. Look at what happened even when Samson lied to Delilah concerning the source of his strength. Delilah disclosed the "secret" to the lords of the Philistines. They believed and brought to her seven fresh bowstrings that had not been dried.

---

4    Chambers, Oswald. *My Utmost for His Highest*. United States: Barbour, 1963.

Delilah did as Samson told her. She tied him up and implemented the hidden scheme of her heart. Samson did not know that Delilah had strategically arranged for the Philistines to be in the back room at that time. When she startled him, Samson broke the cords with ease. She did not get to the secret of his strength but now she knew one thing that could not hold Samson back (Judges 16:6-9).

The second was a deliberate and intentional move. "Delilah said unto Samson, Behold, thou hast mocked me, and told me lies: now tell me, I pray thee, wherewith thou mightest be bound." Again, she did not mince her words, but was forceful. She was on a mission to find out the source of Samson's strength and she wanted to know what could subdue him. Slowly but steadily, she pursued her objective.

On the third attempt, Samson got closer to the source of his strength. "If thou weavest the seven locks of my head with the web," Samson said. Delilah delightedly went beyond weaving the seven braids of his hair in a loom. She tied them up with a pin. Disappointedly, she discovered that it was another trick (Judges 16:13).

On a fourth attempt, Delilah waged psychological warfare as she used the power of her emotions to get to God's chosen servant.

"How canst thou say, I love thee, when thine heart is not with me? thou hast mocked me these three times, and hast not told me wherein thy great strength lieth" (Judges 16:15).

Once you consort with someone and become one flesh it is hard to shake off such emotions.

Knowing that she had backed God's man in a corner, she prodded and nagged him day after day until Samson was exasperated to death.

At his wits' end, he finally yielded and disclosed the secret. Look at how the Word of God lays it out with clarity:

" . . . He told her all his heart, and said unto her, There hath not come a razor upon mine head; for I have been a Nazarite unto God from my mother's womb: if I be shaven, then my strength will go from me, and I shall become weak, and be like any other man.

And when Delilah saw that he had told her all his heart, she sent and called for the lords of the Philistines, saying, Come up this once, for he hath shewed me all his heart. Then the lords of the Philistines came up unto her, and brought money in their hand.

And she made him sleep upon her knees; and she called for a man, and she caused him to shave off the seven locks of his head; and she began to afflict him, and his strength went from him.

And she said, The Philistines be upon thee, Samson. And he awoke out of his sleep, and said, I will go out as at other times before, and shake myself. And he wist not that the Lord was departed from him.

But the Philistines took him, and put out his eyes, and brought him down to Gaza, and bound him with fetters of brass; and he did grind in the prison house." (Judges 16:17-21)

God allowed us to see what went on in Samson's heart by giving us Judges 16:20. There were assumptions. The same assumptions plague God's servants who drift and stray from their calling even today.

What do some of these assumptions look like? In reality, assumptions say:

"I am an anointed servant; God will not take His power from my life. This is my new lifestyle; why should I expect anything to change. I have engaged in these sins for a while but God's touch has remained on my life. Look at the results, don't they testify to God's presence with me? Nothing can take away God's power from my life. Nothing can stop God from working. The God Who chose me knows me."

Assumptions say, "I will go back to it one more time. I will taste it one last time. That will not hurt me or anybody. I will be careful. I will repent once I am done with that."

Look at Samson's assumption.

"I will go out as at other times before, and shake myself. And he wist not that the Lord was departed from him."

Women have been used repeatedly in the world to get to the inner secrets of men's hearts. Women have been part of war plots that foil the plans of the opponent as they disclosed acquired secrets that were used to defeat the enemy.

## Let Us Apply It

In the heat of pleasure, the heart is careless and carefree. Many times, it does not take time to consider the consequences. It does not stop to question or evaluate its motives.

At the apex of indulgences, your heart will not stop to discern the schemes of the enemy. In fact, it is in such moments of deep momentary pleasure and when your heart is wandering away from God that you will disclose what is sacred to the enemy. It is easy to side with the enemy at that point. You will talk of the strengths and what leads to the success of God's work. The very secrets you disclose are what the enemy will use to get to you and to lay strategic obstacles in place to hinder God's work.

Look at the correlation between Samson's narration and God's enumeration of what seduction looks like in Proverbs 7. Look at the warnings. Indeed, no offer from the enemy is worth taking regardless of how good it looks. Conversely, there is no free offer from your adversary. His offers have costly penalties for anyone who accepts them. They are not just baits that lead to destruction and death but will also keep you from God's service.

> "My son, keep my words, and lay up my commandments with thee.
>
> Keep my commandments, and live; and my law as the apple of thine eye.

Bind them upon thy fingers, write them upon the table of thine heart.

Say unto wisdom, Thou art my sister; and call understanding thy kinswoman:

That they may keep thee from the strange woman, from the stranger which flattereth with her words.

For at the window of my house I looked through my casement,

And beheld among the simple ones, I discerned among the youths, a young man void of understanding,

Passing through the street near her corner; and he went the way to her house,

In the twilight, in the evening, in the black and dark night:

And, behold, there met him a woman with the attire of an harlot, and subtil of heart.

(She is loud and stubborn; her feet abide not in her house:

Now is she without, now in the streets, and lieth in wait at every corner.)

So she caught him, and kissed him, and with an impudent face said unto him,

I have peace offerings with me; this day have I payed my vows.

Therefore came I forth to meet thee, diligently to seek thy face, and I have found thee.

I have decked my bed with coverings of tapestry, with carved works, with fine linen of Egypt.

I have perfumed my bed with myrrh, aloes, and cinnamon.

Come, let us take our fill of love until the morning: let us solace ourselves with loves.

For the goodman is not at home, he is gone a long journey:

He hath taken a bag of money with him, and will come home at the day appointed.

With her much fair speech she caused him to yield, with the flattering of her lips she forced him.

He goeth after her straightway, as an ox goeth to the slaughter, or as a fool to the correction of the stocks;

Till a dart strike through his liver; as a bird hasteth to the snare, and knoweth not that it is for his life.

Hearken unto me now therefore, O ye children, and attend to the words of my mouth.

Let not thine heart decline to her ways, go not astray in her paths.

For she hath cast down many wounded: yea, many strong men have been slain by her.

Her house is the way to hell, going down to the chambers of death."

What will it take to accomplish God's work and to display His splendor?

Anyone who desires to do God's work and to accomplish His purposes must be aware of the enemy's schemes. This calls on those who will be servants of the Lord to not only understand their own weakness but to safeguard those potential areas that attract the enemy.

Sexual promiscuity ranks high on the list of untamed passions, but it does not stand alone. Many other passions rob us of God's anointing and power. They leave us empty, naked, and powerless to stand and minister to God's people.

Our generation suffers from endless spiritual plights because of untamed passions. Many anointed servants of God have found themselves off-guard like

Samson. While thinking they will arise and minister, they have found themselves without God's touch, power, and abiding presence. In hopelessness, they have remained buried and chained in the very mire they were anointed to break.

Untamed appetites, addictions, and indulgences of varied types have crippling power. The enemy capitalizes on such compulsions to keep millions enslaved and held under his heavy bondage.

You must understand that the enemy is a schemer. In our generation, he uses good things to keep God's children and servants senseless, blind, and powerless. Many neither know nor understand the extent to which they are chained. Spiritual apathy, defeat, hopelessness, despair, mental and emotional breakdowns are outward telltale signs of the inner networking of the enemy. Family fragmentations, lawlessness, godlessness, and infiltration of sensuality are overt, screaming signs for help.

## What Does the Scheme of the Enemy Look Like?

Let us understand the enemy's scheme for our own modern times.

I would like you to envision a band of disguised armed bandits standing in a circle while leaving an opening for someone to get into the circle. At a distance, there are three salespersons engaging three groups of people in captivating talks. The first salesperson is an attractive woman with whom men are very fascinated. The second is a youthful man in his thirties. He has engaged a group of young people with new models of electronic devices that allow instant communication, collaboration, and associations with friends across the globe. The device has the ability to create live situations that enable you to be part of each other's life experience at the moment. The third person has all kinds of magazines and modern art drawings of nude pictures and obscene work to which another set of individuals are attracted.

Each salesperson keeps each group focused and heavily engrossed with the objects they are selling. What each group does not know is that each salesperson has the objective of getting his group into the circle of armed bandits. Each group is also unaware that among them are individuals who belong to the bandit group. Their role is to give enchanting, exaggerated, and fake testimonies on each object of sale. Their work is to create intense appetite in the members of each group. They do this by changing and presenting different styles, models, and techniques to sustain the fascination. Every member of the group gets a chance to touch, taste, or experience the object of their enthrallment. The tasting is designed to cleverly engage all senses while diminishing the ability for individuals to think or reason on their own. In essence, it blocks them from seeing reality.

Each group does not realize that it is following their salesperson. They are blind to the fact that at great moments of joy, excitement, and allure, the salespersons take backward steps towards the bandits. Following the salesperson is mandatory for anyone who desires to experience maximum pleasure and fulfilment.

Without realizing, each group is carefully led into the circle of bandits. As soon as each individual gets in, he is confronted with the opportunity to settle down, to explore, and to experience the sales' object fully in what looks like the safety of the wall that surrounds him.

No dull moments are allowed in this circle. The minds of those who are captured are kept active, entertained, and looking for the promise of more exciting new deliveries. The circle offers what looks like a fulfilling and desirous life that one can have. You stay in it longer than you would have ever dreamed. While in the circle, you lose focus on important missions in life. You forfeit responsibilities and you take on a careless and carefree attitude. You remain blind to the reality that now you are a prisoner and a captive. You cannot break free from the circle. Only a force stronger than the surrounding army may set you free and allow you to get back to your mission in life.

I find an alarmingly high number of God's beloved children and servants in this circle. Many are chained, entangled, enslaved, and as far removed from their call and mission as you may think.

Satan is smart. He has many clever tricks and schemes for this century. He knows what will keep masses enslaved, entertained, and fascinated while he wreaks havoc in the vineyard of God. He knows how to keep you from your call. He knows how to distract you. He does this by studying what appeals to your appetite. He studies the weaknesses of the multitudes. Some trends are obvious and highly predictable. He has mastered what you cannot resist easily. He knows what to offer. Satan understands how to package it attractively. Your enemy knows for what you will fall. Be careful.

No Christian is too strong for the luring schemes of the enemy. Satan will intensify his tactics the more he realizes that his days are few. He will work overtime to ensure that the once-anointed servants of God come to serve his ugly purposes. Be a wise consumer.

Take time and understand how businesses start and flourish. Before a successful businessperson puts a product out to consumers, he studies the market. He assesses the needs, the appetites, the cravings, and the relevant supporting data. This discloses the type of product to make. He also studies the market. He must ascertain the possibility of good sales. He must know when and where the sales will be optimal. When he finally puts that fancy product on the market, he pushes for sales through varied promotional and marketing strategies. He has to get to the targeted consumer.

Our adversary is engaged in such businesslike deals. He has an objective and he is dedicated to making good sales. He has already identified his target group—Christians. He knows his goal. Every day, he schemes and plans how he must get to his targets. He knows how to execute his plans subtly. He does this with precision at a set time. He is effective. He knows how to mastermind a sensual and pleasure-seeking society. Unfortunately, this does not exclude the church.

Who will step out to meet the needs of our generation?

How will we display God's splendor in our times?

How will we regain what the enemy has taken and destroyed? How can we be effective again in winning the hearts of men and women back to God?

## Activities to Help You Reach Out to Those Who Need Help

The enemy is always on a deadly mission with his adversary. Behind every lure and deceptive scheme is the enemy's desire to take away your spiritual influence. No Christian is too strong for the luring schemes of the enemy.

1. Identify four people who once loved and followed God but now they are cold, discouraged, and/or indifferent?

2. Pray for them every day for one week. Make specific requests to God on their behalf. Among your requests should be tenderness of their hearts to God, a sensitive spirit, a repentant heart, and a willingness to listen to you.

3. Reach out to each of the individuals in the best way possible as you seek to see them restored to God. You can call, send a special message, talk with them, invite them to your house for a talk, or have a meal together.

4. Continue to pray, fellowship, share God's Word, and encourage them. Stand with them until you see them restored to God.

## Memory Verses

*Be sober, be vigilant; because your adversary the devil, as a roaring lion, walketh about, seeking whom he may devour:*

*Whom resist stedfast in the faith, knowing that the same afflictions are accomplished in your brethren that are in the world.*

1 Peter 5:8-9

# Part Two
# What Will It Take to Display God's Splendor?

*Chapter Five*

# What Will It Take to Display God's Splendor in Our Generation?

*I think it is possible for ordinary people to choose to be extraordinary.*

Elon Musk[5]

## Those Who Seek Him Will Display His Splendor

What prompted David to write, "He that dwelleth in the secret place of the Most High shall abide under the shadow of the Almighty" (Psalm 91:1). What kind of rest did the king experience from being in God's presence that made him tell the world about it? As we know, life was not easy in King David's era. David's life was plagued with turmoil, war, and revolt. How did he get to that place of tranquility in spite of his surroundings?

Have you experienced threats from every side in your life? How easy is it to find peace and calmness in tumultuous moments?

When you think about different Bible characters who displayed God's splendor, King David will come to mind. Today, we can get to the presence

---

5    Musk, Elon. "Collecting Innovation Today." Interview by Barry Hurd. The Henry Ford, June 26, 2008. Audio, 06:29. https://www.thehenryford.org/explore/stories-of-innovation/visionaries/elon-musk/#gallery-video=54bmQwMTqtW8ex-6NumdLxJLm3HjEJRC.

of God in true worship and adoration because of the pattern of worship and praise given to us through this special man.  It is not easy for a man to worship when his environment dictates fear, worry, and anxiety.

I cannot help but wonder and ask, "How does a man do that?" What will make a man serve God regardless of his surrounding? How can we get back to serving God? What will it take to serve Him in this generation? How can we display God's splendor amidst our preoccupations? How will we influence others in our times?

David had clear insights for all who will serve God.

Those who will display God's splendor must seek Him.

You see, we are only servants of God. Servants do not carry out their own bidding. They do the will of the master. Good and honorable servants learn to listen to their masters with keenness. This is the only way they can hear and follow instructions. This is a quality that every master desires and cherishes in his servant. Beloved servants stay close to their masters too. It is in staying close that they understand the desires, the wishes, and even the wants of their masters. This is what knits them to the hearts of their masters. True dedication to their service results from their understanding the will and the vision of those they serve.

A servant who remains distant from his master cannot serve him well. Think about this in practical day-to-day life situations. A worker who fully understands his employer's company and vision can steer that business to great success. He does not require much supervision to do that. He can run it effectively and efficiently even in the absence of his employer.

A Christian who desires to serve God and to display His splendor in this generation must seek God. He must hear God. He must understand and do what God says.

As we have noted, this generation is bombarded with endless challenges. No human being has the power or the strength to combat such challenges effectively. It takes God to change the heart of man. As Albert Einstein noted, you cannot solve a problem with the same mind that created it.[6] Those who will effectively deal with the issues and spiritual challenges of our time must have the mindset of God. They will not do it without God's presence or power. They must seek His knowledge, wisdom, understanding, and discernment.

David must have understood this secret in greater depths than we may know or even acknowledge.

Remember, David took over the leadership of Israel from Saul. Saul, the first king of Israel, rose to power at a time of lawlessness. As God points in the book of Judges 17:6 and 21:25, in those days, there was no king in Israel and every man did what was right in his own eyes.

Saul did not take advantage of the anointing of God on his life to restore Israel back to God. Instead, he walked in rebellion and disobedience to God. Israel drifted even further from God during the reign of King Saul.

God wanted Saul to set the children of Israel free from the oppression and bondage of the Amalekites. In 1 Samuel 15, God asked Saul to smite Amalek. He instructed Saul to destroy everything Amalek had, including the inhabitants of their land, oxen, sheep, camels, and asses. However, Saul was snared and entangled by those same things he was asked to destroy.

Saul and his army spared the kings of those lands. They reserved the best of the sheep, oxen, and fat calves for themselves. They destroyed only what was weak and despised—refuse—what was of no consequence (1 Samuel 15:8-9). What Saul did not know was that, in siding with the enemy, he was hurting the people of God. In disobeying God, he was creating a fertile environment for the enemy to inflict and hurt God's chosen children. Saul did not understand the consequences of his actions either. Regardless of the excuses Saul laid before God's prophet, Nathan, for disobeying God, look at God's response to the anointed man who should have delivered Israel from the bondage of their time.

---

6    Havas, Peter., Beck, Anna., Einstein, Albert. *The Collected Papers of Albert Einstein: The Berlin years: Correspondence, January-December 1921 - v. 13. The Berlin years: writings and correspondence, January 1922 - March 1923.* United States: Princeton University Press, 1987.

"And Samuel said, When thou wast little in thine own sight, wast thou not made the head of the tribes of Israel, and the LORD anointed thee king over Israel?

And the Lord sent thee on a journey, and said, Go and utterly destroy the sinners the Amalekites, and fight against them until they be consumed.

Wherefore then didst thou not obey the voice of the Lord, but didst fly upon the spoil, and didst evil in the sight of the Lord?" (1 Samuel 15:17-19).

Just as God reminds all who will serve Him of their importance and origin in 1 Corinthians 1:27, He took Saul back to his roots. When God chose him, Saul was small, unknown, and from a little-known tribe in Israel. Nevertheless, God had anointed him to be king over Israel. The Lord sent Saul on a mission to destroy the wicked enemies of God's people, the Amalekites. Saul's importance and effectiveness lay in obeying and following God.

God rejected Saul as king. He stripped Saul of his honor and power.

"And Saul said unto Samuel, I have sinned: for I have transgressed the commandment of the LORD, and thy words: because I feared the people, and obeyed their voice.

Now therefore, I pray thee, pardon my sin, and turn again with me, that I may worship the LORD.

And Samuel said unto Saul, I will not return with thee: for thou hast rejected the word of the LORD, and the LORD hath rejected thee from being king over Israel.

And as Samuel turned about to go away, he laid hold upon the skirt of his mantle, and it rent.

And Samuel said unto him, The LORD hath rent the kingdom of Israel from thee this day, and hath given it to a neighbour of thine, that is better than thou" (1 Samuel 15:24-28).

Today we also have rulers and governing laws. However, sensuality, carnality, and reckless living have plunged us into a state that is similar to that of Israel at the time of Saul.

Imagine stepping into leadership to take over from Saul.

I believe David's heart must have trembled with fear and holy reverence for the Lord Almighty. As any wise leader, you cannot step into such a position without learning from the mistakes of those who ruled before you.

A good leader would analyze how previous leaders failed and what hindered their success.

When you look at Saul's life, you do not see a man who seeks God or cares to follow His commandments. Instead, Saul embraced his God-given position of leadership but used it to increase his own pride and ambitions.

It is no wonder that David ascended to the throne with fear and reverence. Instead of walking away from God, he sought ways to be close and to maintain an intimate communion. Instead of choosing disobedience like Saul, he chose to obey fully out of love and honor.

David chose to seek God. He made up his mind to understand and to do God's work in God's way. It does not surprise anyone that David became a worshipper of God. He must have understood that there was no way to change or help God's people outside of God's working.

Like Saul, David was not a renowned man before he ascended to the throne. He was neither influential nor wise. He belonged to the crowd that is called and used by God as listed in 1 Corinthians 1:26-29. See if you can identify yourself with this group.

> "For ye see your calling, brethren, how that not many wise men after the flesh, not many mighty, not many noble, are called:
>
> But God hath chosen the foolish things of the world to confound the wise; and God hath chosen the weak things of the world to confound the things which are mighty;

And base things of the world, and things which are despised, hath God chosen, yea, and things which are not, to bring to nought things that are:

That no flesh should glory in his presence."

## Let Us Apply It to Our Times

You will affect the spiritual situations of our times by seeking God. Those who desire to affect our generation in godly and positive ways must learn to seek God. If it were up to us to produce desirable changes in the lives of men and women, we could not have done it positively. Most leaders have tried this for a long time. We are equipped with the latest technologies, researches, plans, methods, facilities, and even funds to combat current problems that plague our lives. However, the results reveal our inabilities and ineffectiveness. Every day sees more people plunged in despair and hopelessness. The complexities of the crises of life keep leaders on their toes in search of answers.

What does this tell us? What does it reveal regarding the complexities of man's problems?

1. It could mean that we are ill-equipped to meet the needs of our times.
2. It could also point to the reality that we have the wrong diagnosis of what man's problems could be.
3. This could be an indication that we are unable to effectively solve our own problems and therefore we need help.

I believe that all these statements are true.

There is one reality we must face. Most of what manifests in society as physical, emotional, and psychological turmoil have deep spiritual roots. Just as it is hard to treat a physical problem with a spiritual solution, it is equally hard to meet the spiritual needs of a society through physical solutions. I am afraid this is the seedbed that cultures, incubates, and multiplies our maladies beyond control.

When you chop off your fingers at work, you pray and ask God to help you as you make your way to the doctors. You don't stand there praying against Satan or his demons for causing the injury as you bleed to death. On the other hand, when your heart is in turmoil because of sin and your conscience is plagued from your actions, indulgences, and bad choices, no physical solution will restore peace and rest to your soul. You may exercise, seek counsel, get a diagnosis for a common malady, or even take medication. These physical interventions, however effective and wonderful, may not solve the problem.

Many societies today are dealing with deep-rooted spiritual problems for which they offer wonderful physical solutions.

Nothing is known to change man like the power of God. God and His Word have an incomprehensible ability to not only diagnose man's problem but to effectively bring healing and restore man to a life of peace, joy, and rest.

The word of God is quick, and powerful, and sharper than any two-edged sword, piercing even to the dividing asunder of soul and spirit, and of the joints and marrow. It dissects precisely to the extent of discerning the thoughts and intents of the heart (Hebrews 4:12).

God's Word brings healing and wholeness (Psalm 107:20). His Word gives life (Proverbs 4:20-22). God gives peace and rest (Isaiah 26:3-4).

Wholeness, Peace, Quietness, Rest—these are words that are foreign in our generation. However, this is what God desires for His children.

Those whose who will seek God will point this generation to His healing balm. The challenges of our times must be combated by the extraordinary divine power of God. That is because true change springs from a transformed heart. Empty words do not effect lasting change. Physical programs and methods, however revised and refined, have limitations. Our generation is crying out for help and only those who seek, hear, and follow God will lead men and women to meaningful and lasting solutions from their sorrows.

Those who will not seek God will not only fail to help this generation but will find themselves entangled in the very quirk mires for which they were born to solve. You are entrusted with divine treasures for times such as these. Will you seek God? God wants you to display His splendor in this generation.

## Activities to Help You Step Out to Display the Splendor of God

A servant who remains distant from his master cannot serve him well. Our generation is crying out for help and only those who seek, hear, and follow God will lead men and women to meaningful and lasting solutions from their sorrows.

1. In what ways has God blessed and gifted you for His service?
2. Where and how can you use your gifts and blessings to serve God?
3. Take time this week to seek God earnestly concerning what He will have you do with His gifts in your life. Ask Him to stand with you so you can minister and serve in His power. Increase your time in prayer as you seek Him each day for the entire week.
4. In what ways can you use what you have to reach out and help those whom God brings into your life?

### Memory Verse

*But the people that do know their God shall be strong, and do exploits.*

Daniel 11:32b

## Chapter Six

# Dwelling in the Secret Place of the Almighty

*I desire many things concerning myself; but I desire nothing so much as to have a heart filled with love to the Lord. I long for a warm personal attachment to Him.*

George Muller[7]

## Dwelling in the Secret Place

What does it even mean to dwell in the secret place of the Almighty God? What does God mean when He says, "He that dwelleth in the secret place of the most High shall abide under the shadow of the Almighty" (Psalm 91:1).

When I was in high school, we had some rare days when the president visited our school. Those were special moments. We eagerly awaited those occasions with great anticipation and preparation. On the day of his visitation, you sought to sit or stand in positions that put you in conspicuous locations.

The president was unpredictable. He was known to call on any student to answer strategically-planned questions that pointed to the needs of the school. You had to be ready, alert, and at your best.

---

7    Müller, George. *A Narrative of Some of the Lord's Dealings with George Müller*. United States: January 15, 2007.

It was fascinating to meet the president. While he addressed the school community, we gave him our undivided attention out of loyalty. We listened intently and committed to memory everything he said. We fastened our eyes on him so much that we forgot about everything and everyone else who surrounded us for a moment. Distractions had no place in those solemn assemblies. We were delighted to be in his presence, and we cherished every minute. We took him for his word, and none of us wanted to see those special moments end.

At the end of it all, we walked away with a new spring in our steps. We walked with pride. Who could make light of such moments? After all, not many schools had the privilege of interacting with the president.

We rehearsed the president's speech and held to his promises. It was hard to shut up as we competed to see who would accurately repeat his words. We basked in the joy and excitement of the moment for days, if not months. There were greater implications for those visits than we originally thought. They seemed to set us on a pedestal, separating us from the rest of the students whose schools were never visited. It is true that we felt special. However, it left us with responsibilities. There was an inner urge to set a good example. It also birthed in us a desire for excellence. How else could we prove our belief of being special if we had nothing to show for it?

Today, as I reflect on those innocent days, I see a similarity of what it means to dwell in the secret place of the Almighty. Just as we delighted in the company of the president, Christians can delight in the presence of the Lord. We can linger and enjoy every moment. While with Him, you can shift your focus from everything else and give Him your undivided attention. Christians can fasten their spiritual eyes on God as they enjoy His beauty. We can hungrily listen to every word He speaks. We can rehearse, believe, and act on each word, knowing that He is not a man that should lie, nor the Son of Man that should repent. We can walk out of His presence and yet live in the splendor of that fellowship before we seek more communion.

Our interaction with God truly sets us on that spiritual pedestal of special and peculiar people—the people of God—a chosen generation—a holy priesthood (1 Peter 2:9-10).

Dwelling in God's presence as you gaze on His beauty draws you into an intimate relationship with Him. It creates loyalty. You delight to serve Him out of love.

God's children who get to this point in their lives seek opportunities to behold the face of their Master. They create meaningful moments where they sit at His feet to listen and get instructions for their everyday lives. They hesitate to move or act without God's assurance. They seek to hear and to know Him. When they step away from God's throne of grace, they display His splendor. As they act on God's instructions, they execute their duties with the touch and favor of God. They influence people in specific and unique ways.

You see, no one ever dwells in the presence of the Lord and remains the same. There is no one person who has sought God wholeheartedly and remained unchanged. When Moses gazed upon God's face for forty days and nights, he radiated God's glory in an unfamiliar way. Then when he descended from Mount Sinai after lingering in God's presence while Yahweh inscribed the Ten Commandments on tablets, his face glowed. Those who saw Moses could not look on the glorious reflection of God as his face shined. So much was the brilliance and radiance that Moses had to cover his face with a veil (Exodus 34:29-35).

Those who saw the radiance on Moses' face experienced something that was more than a mere reflection. What was it that made them afraid? Why did they retreat as he approached them? Why didn't they want Moses to speak to them directly?

## The Source of the Shine

When you dwell in God's presence, He shines His face on you and you display His power and anointing. The shine is not a fabricated luster. It is a reflection of the very person of God, and a guaranteed deposit of His indwelling strength with outward manifestations.

The mighty works that Moses did in the name of the Lord are a testament to this indwelling presence of God. No human being, however strong, skilled, or gifted, could lead millions of people through that treacherous wilderness. It took the mighty hand of God. This means that those with whom God entrusted the responsibility of leading and shepherding His people had to depend on God. They had to walk with Him and obey His instructions. That is the only way they were able to display God's splendor.

Look at the life of the man to whom God revealed the secret of displaying divine splendor. What was David's day like? What did he do above the ordinary and average man of his day? Why did God love him? Is it a wonder that God chose David's family to display both spiritual and physical splendor?

As you go back to Psalm 91:1, you see David referring to dwelling in the secret place. Dwelling is different from visiting. To dwell is to linger with delight. It is to cherish the place so much that you wish to stay there forever. To dwell carries with it the connotation of a safe and lovely place. A place you love to live. It has an aspect of permanency and ownership. With this thought in mind, it makes sense that those who dwell in the secret place abide under the shadow of the Almighty. When you like where you are and you are lingering as long as you can, you stay there by choice and enjoy the honor and privilege of the place. You also do everything in your power to remain there.

Look at how the man who dwelled in the secret place arrived there. His heart got there long before his feet took him there. He carried the special place in his heart and lived by the joys and affections of that amazing place.

God has disclosed the heart of those who seek to display His glory in Psalm 42:1-2. Try to envision David in these lines. "As the hart panteth after the water brooks, so panteth my soul after thee, O God. My soul thirsteth for God, for the living God: when shall I come and appear before God?"

Look at the deep longing of David's soul. Such an overwhelming gravitation of the heart toward God does not leave a man or a woman the same. This is a desire that demands action and witnesses immense results.

It doesn't come as a surprise, then, to find the same man saying, "I was glad when they said unto me, Let us go into the house of the LORD" (Psalm 122:1).

Look at the time David got to the secret place of the Almighty. It was early. He made it a daily priority and made the most of it as depicted in Psalm 63:1-2. "O God, thou art my God; early will I seek thee: my soul thirsteth for thee, my flesh longeth for thee in a dry and thirsty land, where no water is; To see thy power and thy glory, so as I have seen thee in the sanctuary."

It is no wonder that Solomon, David's own son, would write saying, "I love them that love me; and those that seek me early shall find me" (Proverbs 8:17). I guess you cannot remain the same when surrounded by a man who seeks the Lord. Solomon must have been a first-hand witness of the impact of seeking God in his father's life.

It was from such seeking that the great man of God obtained power and saw God's glory. You cannot display what you do not have.

The longer I live, the more I realize that life does not offer anything freely. It is true that there is no such thing as free lunch. Someone has to pay for the meal. This is also true when it comes to spiritual matters. Salvation is free to the believer, but Christ still pays for the meal in this case.

We receive God's gift of salvation by grace through faith. It is free, but spiritual victory and power to live a victorious and fruitful life demand action.

As you approach God in faith, believing and trusting Him to commune with you, He responds in accordance to His Word and does exactly that. He rewards those who diligently seek Him (Hebrews 11:6). The greatest reward God can give those who seek Him is the privilege of walking and serving in His power as they display His splendor.

Those who sit in chains and under the bondage of the enemy need help. Someone must call on God on their behalf. Those who are addicted and harassed by the enemy day and night desire change and victory, too. If they had power to set themselves free, they could. Someone must fight on their behalf. The chains that bind humanity today will be liberated only in response to the power of God.

Those who will effectively minister to the unique needs of our generation are the men and women who will display the splendor of God. Those who will make a difference in the lives of people must seek God.

God is available to all His children in equal measures. You can have as much of God in your life as you desire. Any of God's children can display His glory with great magnitude. You just have to get to the secret place and dwell and delight in it.

God's promises still stand for those who desire to make a difference in our world today. You do not have to walk through life empty and powerless. You can seek Him. You can display His splendor.

I know you have heard many promises from God but allow me to remind you that God means what He says. His promise in Matthew 7:7-11 is for you. Believe God and let Him equip you to meet the needs of our time.

> Ask, and it shall be given you; seek, and ye shall find; knock, and it shall be opened unto you:
>
> For every one that asketh receiveth; and he that seeketh findeth; and to him that knocketh it shall be opened.
>
> Or what man is there of you, whom if his son ask bread, will he give him a stone?
>
> Or if he ask a fish, will he give him a serpent?
>
> If ye then, being evil, know how to give good gifts unto your children, how much more shall your Father which is in heaven give good things to them that ask him?

## Activities to Establish You in Your Service with God

Dwelling in God's presence as you gaze on His beauty draws you into an intimate relationship with Him. It creates loyalty. You delight to serve Him out of love.

1. Take inventory of your Christian life and service to God. How effective are you in ministering to others?

2. Do you become wearied, faint or discouraged easily?

3. Are you powerless, strengthless, and unfruitful?

4. Get back to the habit of listening and hearing from God. This is the source of your strength and power. Make time every day to pray and to develop a relationship with God. Make time to feed on God's Word every day. Make every session meaningful and productive.

### Memory Verse

*He that dwelleth in the secret place of the most High*
*shall abide under the shadow of the Almighty.*

Psalm 91:1

*Chapter Seven*

# Seeking God

*The first thing to be concerned about was not how much I might serve the Lord, or how I might glorify the Lord; but how I might get my soul into a happy state, and how my inner man might be nourished.*

George Muller[8]

## How Do You Seek God?

How can a mortal human being seek an immortal—spiritual—God?

What exactly does seeking God mean?

Does God listen to human beings? Can He respond powerfully to those who seek Him? What does seeking Him look like? Can God delight in a man? Can He manifest Himself to someone? How many times can one pray to God? Will you not run out of content for prayer?

Should you find yourself asking any of these questions, trust that you are in good company.

Seeking God is not a man-made endeavor. God wants His people to seek Him. He has outlined a path for those who desire to know and to follow Him closely.

---

8    Müller, George. *The Autobiography of George Müller.* United Kingdom: Nisbet/Bible & Tract Warehouse, 1914.

Let us look at what God has revealed and laid out in His Word regarding seeking Him.

To seek Him starts with a simple desire. Every Christian has an inherent desire to follow God. God creates this desire in you at your time of conversion. Non-believers have a desire to know God, too. Man is born with a desire to worship. God reveals Himself to mankind through creation every day. According to Romans 1:19-20, God does not complicate things for those who desire to know Him. He displays His majestic qualities in simple and clear terms for anyone to see, believe, and follow Him. His eternal power and divine nature clearly testify of His existence. They tell of His presence, power, and majesty. They point man to God. He has intentionally set it in this fashion so that man is without an excuse.

Those who follow their God-given desire to seek and know God find Him. Christians who follow the promptings of God in their hearts to draw close to Him find Him. God intertwined this desire within the phenomenon of growth. The more you desire to know and commune with Him, the deeper the desire grows. The more you step out to seek God the thirstier you become and the closer you are drawn to Him.

Remember, this is the desire King David expressed as he likened his spiritual thirst to a deer in desperate need of water (Psalm 42:1). Imagine the reactions of a thirsty deer upon getting to a water source. Think about the deep spiritual pleasure your hungry and thirsty soul feels as you encounter God. Such a soul delights in lingering and gazing upon the beauty of God. After all, doesn't the heart of man seek after deep pleasure and satisfaction? Why would such a fulfilled heart be in a hurry to walk away from the fountain of fulfillment?

It is true that those who seek God with all their hearts find Him. His promise through the Prophet Jeremiah is true even today. "And ye shall seek me, and find me, when ye shall search for me with all your heart. And I will be found of you, saith the LORD: and I will turn away your captivity, and I will gather you from all the nations, and from all the places whither I have driven you, saith the LORD; and I will bring you again into the place whence I caused you to be carried away captive" (Jeremiah 29:13-14).

## What Does Seeking God Look Like?

Imagine that you have two favorite lambs. One evening, you leisurely watch your lambs graze in the backyard as you delight in their beauty. However, your neighbor walks by and you talk for a while. As your neighbor leaves, you remember the lambs. You turn around only to find one lamb. You quickly put that one lamb in the sheep pen and embark to look for the missing one. As you search, you have one consolation—the little lamb cannot be far away. You just saw it a little while ago. You know what it looks like and so spotting it cannot be hard either. However, your fear is how to find it should it lie down in the tall grass or bean patch. You must get this little lamb before dark. What do you do?

You decide to do two things. One, to follow clues, and two, to call out for the lamb. You look for footprints and any patterns in the grass and in the bean field. Since lambs are small and don't leave very obvious footprints, you keenly follow any lead; and as you make sounds to alert the lamb of your presence, the little animal responds. Its little *baa* sound takes you right to where it lies quietly in the tall grass. You happily carry the lamb home and talk about it for the rest of the evening.

Now, go through the steps that led to your finding the little lamb as we apply it to seeking and finding God.

First, you realized that you were missing something. It wasn't just anything useless or valueless. You were missing something that was dear to you. Its absence would affect you in some ways.

Second, you wanted your lamb back. You would not sit or go through the night without knowing where the lamb was. It did not take planning, formulating a committee, or calling on friends to accompany you on your search for it. You followed your natural instincts and without a word to anyone or making a scene out of it, you set out to get the lamb.

Third, you went searching for the lamb. You did not sit to wait for the poor little thing to get back on its own. You cared. You took a step.

Fourth, your search was diligent, intentional, and targeted. You knew where to look. You knew how to follow clues. You knew what it would take to get the lamb, and you did it.

Seeking God takes a similar path.

You come to a point when you realize you are missing something, and it holds great value. You cannot live without it. As you come to that realization, you know exactly what it means to have God close. You can reminiscence on God's goodness and the fulfillment that comes from His closeness. As you look at your current spiritual situation, you recognize the emptiness, the lack of fulfillment, the absence of God's voice and direction. You get tired of the void and the lukewarmness of your heart.

This emptiness and apathy create a desire for God. Your heart develops a hunger, and you decide to make a move to find God. This is because you do not want to go through the night hours of your life without Him. You know what an anchor He is and the difference He will make in your life.

It is hard to settle for crumbs when you have once sat at table with God and enjoyed the bounty of His love and fellowship. It is tough to go through dark nights alone while distant from God. There is nothing in the world that can compare to God's comfort and encouragement as He speaks strength to your heart in the most troubled times of your life. The hope, peace, and inner calmness are a few of the unexplainable treasures with which He fills your soul.

The thought of what you could have sends you on a quest to search for God. That inner cry and deep desire lead you to practical ways to get close to Him. Just like in the case of our little lamb, you look for practical ways to get to Him. You look at where He has been. You look at what He has done, and you go for Him as you make your search diligent, intentional, and targeted. You call on Him and tune in to hear Him. You search for Him in places you are sure to find Him. You dig into His Holy Word and incline your eyes to His Word.

Please note that seeking God on the other hand is not exactly like looking for a lost lamb. You never get to God like one who finally finds the lamb, only to exclaim with jubilance, "Hey, I found Him."

The very moment you set your heart to seek after God, God begins to unfold and reveal Himself to you. In fact, God helps you find Him. He embraces those who seek Him. For every step you take towards Him, He moves closer to you than you may realize. He ministers to your heart, gives you inner strength, answers prayers, and comes through in significant ways to encourage your heart. This is part of His revelation to you. Such revelation acts like fuel to keep your quest for Him going. He keeps revealing and showing Himself to you as you continue to walk, talk, and listen to Him. Before you know it, you will trust and develop a fondness for Him more. You will find Him a true friend that you must have. You will find His presence real. You will identify His voice better. You will delight to hear Him. You will be fulfilled to obey Him. Above all, you will cherish a close walk with Him.

It is at this point when He gets so real that your fellowship transitions from a time of just asking of Him in prayer to a time of worship. It is at this point, too, that your heart delights to be in His presence. You enjoy gazing upon His face as you appreciate Him for Who He is. You will be satisfied to spend quality time with Him. Your heart will not be bothered if you did not make a single request in those precious moments. Finally, you will not even know that you are displaying His splendor and being a help to His people.

The closest I can come to explaining this is to take you back to the time you were in deep love. Think about the pleasure of being in the company of someone you love. Imagine the beauty, the joy, the thrill of just gazing at them. You do not have to say a word for them to know you love them. Imagine the anticipation of meeting. What about the joy and the thrill of strolling in the park, just the two of you?

This may make you understand the emotions that were in David's heart as he wrote Psalm 27:4.

> "One thing have I desired of the LORD, that will I seek after; that I may dwell in the house of the LORD all the days of my life, to behold the beauty of the LORD, and to enquire in his temple."

What kind of desires can a man have to warrant such writing? What emotions fill a heart to want God this badly? More importantly, how does the Great God of the universe respond to such a person?

Imagine the rejoicing your heart goes through when you find your lost lamb before dark. Imagine the calmness that fills your heart as you lay your head down in sweet sleep. Now imagine what it means to go through life with God. Imagine the confidence and tranquility with which He fills and satisfies your life.

It is no wonder David likened it to a heart panting like a deer for a drink of water. A heart can only pant that way for real treasure. How many times does your heart long and thirst for change? The heart has unbelievable power and potential to fight for what is valuable.

You, too, will find Him when you seek Him with all of your heart. You will find Him when your heart wants Him. You will find Him when you diligently go for Him. "You will seek me and find me when you seek me with all of your heart."

## Activities to Help You Walk on God's Trail

Those who follow their God-given desire to seek and know God find Him. Christians who follow the promptings of God in their hearts to draw close to Him find Him.

Take an honest look at your life and apply this litmus test to see if your heart is suffering from spiritual malnutrition, which comes because of spending too little or no time with God.

1.  Is your heart hungry and empty? Are you searching for what you do not know?

2.  Does your life lack true joy and inner peace?

3.  Are you constantly anxious, restless, and uncertain on what to do most of the time?

4.  Are you seemingly floating around not sure how, when, or even where to fit in your service to God?

5.  Is your relationship with God shallow, inconsistent, and superficial?

God desires to have a strong and intimate relationship with you. Start cultivating it today. Get back to reading and studying His Word. Pray and ask Him to help you pray every day. Ask Him to take away the lack of desire and sluggishness of spirit. Instead, pray for a spiritual appetite and a desire for Him. Do this consistently for the next seven days.

## Memory Verses

*And ye shall seek me, and find me, when ye shall search for me with all your heart. And I will be found of you, saith the LORD: and I will turn away your captivity, and I will gather you from all the nations, and from all the places whither I have driven you, saith the LORD; and I will bring you again into the place whence I caused you to be carried away captive.*

Jeremiah 29:13-14

## Chapter Eight

# The Transformation of Spending Time with God

*Our greatest fear should not be of failure,*
*but of succeeding at something that doesn't really matter.*

D. L. Moody[9]

## Imagine What Spending Time with Him Will Do

Some of the greatest transformations known to occur in man come from spending time with God. When you take a person through psychotherapy, you expect results. You expect to see changes. When you make mistakes and end up in correction centers, the government desires to see certain changes. A prison not only keeps you in check but also provides structure and opportunities for change. When you train a child, you formulate character and so you anticipate change, too. Most of the changes in these scenarios are not permanent. How many times have you seen a process that once brought change repeated multiple times with similar results? How many times have you seen people walk out of prison only to commit a similar or worse crime?

---

9    Moody, Dwight L. *Moody's Last Sermons*. United States: Moody Publishers, 2013.

However, I have seen God work at the heart of man with astounding, lasting results. Those who spend time with God cannot lack desirable changes.

Take the twelve disciples for instance. Think of how long Christ our Savior stayed with them. It took only three and a half years to transform those men. That is because, whereas man works to shape character, Christ transforms the heart. He starts on the inside before getting to the outside. With a transformed heart come new passions, likes, desires, and pursuits.

God chose to work with men who had little formal education and training. For three and a half years, He spent time with them. He taught, trained, shaped, and molded them, revealing Himself to them and transforming their lives.

Think about it.

How long does it take to train children before they can stand on their own and make significant changes in this world? How much counseling does one require to ensure notable changes in one's life?

The three and a half years brought significant changes in every aspect of the disciples' lives. Look at the reactions of those who knew them before their spending those years with Christ.

> "Now when they saw the boldness of Peter and John, and perceived that they were unlearned and ignorant men, they marvelled; and they took knowledge of them, that they had been with Jesus" (Acts 4:13).

> "Look at what the noble and respected men of the land thought of the disciples as they desired to prosecute them. These were the priests, the captain of the temple, and the Sadducees" (Acts 4:1).

> "But when they had commanded them to go aside out of the council, they conferred among themselves, Saying, What shall we do to these men? for that indeed a notable miracle hath been done by them is manifest to all them that dwell in Jerusalem; and we cannot deny it" (Acts 4:15-16).

Imagine, the prosecutors withdrew the disciples from the hearing with the Sanhedrin to discuss and share opinions amongst themselves first.

Imagine those men huddled together, asking, "What shall we do with these men? They are not ordinary anymore. Everyone in Jerusalem knows the great works and signs they have worked in this our region." I like their last thought: "And we cannot deny it."

Despite the charges they laid on the disciples, they acknowledged that God's chosen vessels were different. They were changed. Transformed. They displayed God's splendor for all to see. None failed to see it. Look at the transformations that took place from being with Christ.

- From timid, backward, and untrained men, Peter and John emerged into bold men who spoke to thousands of hearers, to the teachers of the law, to rulers, to the priests, to elders, and even to the high priest.
- From unschooled men, the disciples emerged as intellectual debaters who displayed knowledge, wisdom, and comprehension that astonished the learned and all who listened to them.
- From undesired men who held low and despised jobs in society, many people gathered to listen and to seek the eternal treasures that also made a difference in their lives. They received the miracles they performed. They enjoyed soundness of health, and delighted in the well-being of the family members they brought to the disciples (Acts 3:1-10).
- From foolish men, the disciples became wise. They shocked crowds as they displayed wisdom and discernment.
- From the least esteemed people, the disciples were envied. In fact, it was that jealousy and envy that thrust many of the disciples into prisons and dungeons.

I can only liken this scenario to that kid who was always looked down upon in middle or high school because everyone thought they were better.

Don't we like to compare and draw satisfaction from being better than someone? We part ways with such classmates and never hear about them for years. When we meet after twenty years, our old minds are shocked at what we see. The advancements and the success of the very people we despised in our heart humble us. We are forced to swallow our pride and find out how they made it. As we look at our life struggles, we cannot help but recall our actions to that classmate back in middle school. For you, this may be a true and practical scenario at work as you evaluate your interaction and working with co-workers for years.

The changes in the lives of the disciples did not just affect people momentarily. They had eternal results. We have yet to see many of them. Only eternity will reveal them all. The great news is that every Christian today is a recipient of the outflowing blessings of spending time with God.

## You, Too, Can Display His Splendor by Spending Time with Him

Let me bring your attention back to the big picture. Why are we seeking God? Why do you need His touch and power? It is because those who do not seek God operate in the flesh and in their own strength. This does not yield desired results. The needs that surround us in society can be combated effectively only by the power of God. If you do not seek Him, you will be calloused and indifferent to the needs that await your action.

Seek Him in prayer. God is found by those who spend time with Him in prayer. Look at His promise to you once again from Matthew 7:7-8.

> "Ask, and it shall be given you; seek, and ye shall find; knock, and it shall be opened unto you:
>
> For every one that asketh receiveth; and he that seeketh findeth; and to him that knocketh it shall be opened."

Just as it happened to the disciples, seeking God will transform your life. People will not fail to see the changes that accompany those who seek Him.

When Daniel made up his mind to seek God at the time King Nebuchadnezzar demanded a revelation to what he dreamed, God displayed His splendor through His servant. When all magicians, wise men, soothsayers, astrologers, and the witches of Babylon could not tell the dream to the king, there was only one decree. The king was ready to kill those who enjoyed that favored position as advisors and vision bearers. Unfortunately, Daniel was counted in that group because of his high advisory position to the king.

However, God's servant knew how to find God in those dark hours of life. See Daniel's plan as recorded in Daniel 2:16-19.

> "Then Daniel went in, and desired of the king that he would give him time, and that he would shew the king the interpretation.
>
> Then Daniel went to his house, and made the thing known to Hananiah, Mishael, and Azariah, his companions:
>
> That they would desire mercies of the God of heaven concerning this secret; that Daniel and his fellows should not perish with the rest of the wise men of Babylon.
>
> Then was the secret revealed unto Daniel in a night vision. Then Daniel blessed the God of heaven."

God always comes through for those who seek Him. God does not turn a deaf ear to those who call and seek His face. If He did, He would be a liar. All His promises would be untrustworthy. God answered Daniel and his three friends. He revealed the dream in a night vision and saved their lives.

It is no wonder Daniel broke into high praise and worship as he bragged about God. That is what happens when you seek Him and He is found of you. You cannot help but love Him. Praise is the automatic outpouring of a thankful heart. Look at the heart of a worshipper who seeks God as evidenced in Daniel's praise in Daniel 2:20-23.

"Daniel answered and said, Blessed be the name of God for ever and ever: for wisdom and might are his:

And he changeth the times and the seasons: he removeth kings, and setteth up kings: he giveth wisdom unto the wise, and knowledge to them that know understanding:

He revealeth the deep and secret things: he knoweth what is in the darkness, and the light dwelleth with him.

I thank thee, and praise thee, O thou God of my fathers, who hast given me wisdom and might, and hast made known unto me now what we desired of thee: for thou hast now made known unto us the king's matter."

Those who seek God worship Him, and those who worship know how to seek God. Worship is a declaration of God's faithfulness as you encounter Him in your daily walk, your interactions and communion. Worship is an overflow of Who God is to you on the inside. The lips cannot contain or suppress the deep workings of God in your heart.

Do you desire to affect our generation in a positive way? Do you long to be used by God to meet the needs of our time? Is your heart touched by the distress that characterizes this century? Seek Him. Don't wait! Begin today. Let God draw you to Himself as He unfolds the path to doing it.

## Activities to Help You Serve God's Purposes in This Generation

Does your heart beat with a desire to witness change in our generation? Does the distress and the hopelessness you see in society bring sadness to your heart? Do you long to be used of God to meet the needs of our times? Seek Him.

1.   The secret of having power with God is worship. God inhabits the praises of His people. Make it a point to spend the first ten minutes of your prayer time worshiping and thanking God for Who and What He is in your life.

2. Use prayer effectively to reach out to your community and nation in positive and significant ways. Pray for your leaders. Pray for those who do not know God. Pray for the underprivileged and those with diverse needs.

3. Present yourself as a vessel for use to God. Ask Him to show you what He wants you to do for Him. Ask Him to make His daily appointments of service clear to you.

4. Ask Him for His transforming touch, power, and presence that you may be effective in your service to Him.

## Memory Verses

*And such as do wickedly against the covenant shall he corrupt by flatteries: but the people that do know their God shall be strong, and do exploits.*

Daniel 11:32


*They that go down to the sea in ships, that do business in great waters; These see the works of the LORD, and his wonders in the deep.*

Psalm 107:23-24

Chapter Nine

# What Will It Take to Display His Splendor?

*How far you go in life depends on your being tender with the young,*
*compassionate with the aged, sympathetic with the striving and tolerant of the*
*weak and strong. Because someday in your life you will have been all of these.*

George Washington Carver[10]

## Only Those Who Purpose in Their Hearts
## Will Display His Splendor

I would like you to think of an accomplishment in your life that brings joy and fulfillment to your heart. What did it take for you to complete it? What are your favorite memories about it?

Now take a moment to remember how it all started. Most likely, it first began as a thought. You pondered it, until finally you stepped out to act on it.

When you look at the big accomplishments in people's lives, you are amazed that most of them started off as simple thoughts. Those thoughts were groomed, nurtured, and formulated into projects. Once the heart

---

10   Carver, George Washington., Kremer, Gary R.. *George Washington Carver: In His Own Words*. United Kingdom: University of Missouri Press, 1987.

was convinced and determined to embark on the project, more ideas were generated which in turn mapped a path to success. Once their hearts were convinced of the possible outcome of their project, they stood for it, gave it their best effort, and started off on their road to success.

Displaying God's splendor takes the same plan. Just as any project requires planning, putting in hard work, and overcoming challenges before it will succeed, so does displaying the splendor of God.

Around 605 B.C., Nebuchadnezzar, the king of Babylon, besieged Jerusalem. He was a great leader in command of a strong army. Jerusalem fell into the hands of Nebuchadnezzar, not just because of the strength of this leader but because Judah was under God's judgement for their disobedience.

Characteristic of a powerful army when it raids a territory, Jerusalem was plundered; its inhabitants captured. Among those captured was a fine young man called Daniel.

In those days, when a king invaded and fought against a nation, he took advantage of his defeat in different ways. One common way was to take everything of value; the treasure of the land. That included minerals, spices, animals, and people who were taken as slaves. Whatever was deemed useless and could not be transported was destroyed by fire or by the edge of the sword.

Kings took advantage of their superiority to identify talented and elite individuals among those captured to benefit their own lands. Daniel fell in this category. As a young man from a royal family with high aptitude, Daniel caught the attention of the king's officers. Together with other young men, Daniel was selected to serve in the king's palace. Ordinary people were not chosen to serve in such royal positions. The young men had to qualify based on their descent, good looks, giftedness in knowledge and wisdom, and a high intellectual ability to learn.

As much as this was a coveted position because of the advantage of receiving good royal treatment and later sitting on the advisory council for the king, it had major challenges for those whose hearts beat with the desire to serve and to follow God.

The sumptuous delicacies to which they treated the young men were defiled food served on the king's table. Such food was first offered to idols before the royal court and high-ranking officials could dine.

Daniel and his three friends found themselves in a predicament even as they entered royal service. Would they serve and stay true to Yahweh, the One and Only true God of Israel, or would they surrender their will to bow and partake of that which was shared with idols—pagan gods who could neither hear nor speak?

At face value, this does not seem like a hard decision to make. But remember, these were young prisoners. Daniel was no older than the mid-teenage boy you know. What an honor to be in the king's royal courts at such an age in a foreign country. To succumb to the wishes of the king meant enjoying the favor, protection, privileges, and even the delicacies of King Nebuchadnezzar.

The opposite was also true. To revolt against the order of the king meant slavery, bondage, hard labor, and even death.

Today, we would not read about Daniel in the Holy Scriptures in such a context had he not purposed to display God's splendor. Look at the feeble yet bold steps he took in the palace of the most powerful man on earth.

"But Daniel purposed in his heart that he would not defile himself with the portion of the king's meat, nor with the wine which he drank: therefore he requested of the prince of the eunuchs that he might not defile himself" (Daniel 1:8).

Imagine, your fifteen-year-old son is captured and taken to a foreign country. He is cut off from family and everything familiar, then receives divine favor in that land to enter into training and service at the king's palace. He can decide to follow the king's orders and stay at the place under the king's own protection or to protest his new coveted position, go against the orders of the king, and be put to death.

Daniel, Shadrach, Meshach, and Abednego purposed to honor the great God of heaven. This was the God Who delivered His people out of their land of bondage. This was the Yahweh Who divided the Red Sea and caused His chosen tribe to escape the wrath of Pharaoh. Now, they had an opportunity to stand for the God Who destroyed the entire army of Egypt by drowning everyone in the Rea Sea.

To eat from King Nebuchadnezzar's table was to be defiled before God. It was to disobey God's law as set in Leviticus 11 regarding what and what not to eat and even how to prepare food according to the Mosaic regulations.

To eat what was offered to idols was to recognize and acknowledge that idols—the work of men's hands—were celestial, divine, and even immortal. It was to give them deity and to equate them to God. How far from the truth could that be!

Christians are called to stand for what is right and to be a light in the world. Regardless of who you are, where you are, or what you do, God gives each one of us a chance to display His splendor every day.

Standing for God does not begin with that giant step with cameras and many eyes focused on you. Displaying God's splendor starts with a mere statement of purpose in the heart of the believer. It starts with walking with God, experiencing His deep love and making up your mind to honor Him out of love in those moments when you must choose between Him and the world. It is not easy to say yes to God before the crowds, the cameras, or numerous eyes when it is already hard do so when you are alone. Do not wait for a big stage to accept it, because then you may never do it.

## So How Do You Display His Splendor in Your Day?

God is a God of order. He is meticulous in all He does. That includes placing His children in strategic locations and places at specific times to display His glory. God holds all creation in consistent harmony. He has every piece in the right place and playing its part to ensure the proper running of the universe. He does this so that man can enjoy creation. This way, His children will be satisfied and contented. In turn, they worship their Maker.

Now think about the love God has for man. He created him in His own image to display His glory and splendor. How can God not be intricate in making sure man is in the right place at the right time to fulfill his purpose on earth? God uses people to take care of people. He uses you and me to take care of the needs of our brothers and sisters.

How do you do it?

Where can you display God's splendor?

Let us look at practical ways to do it starting from this very moment.

## 1. Honor God regardless of where you are.

The greatest way man can display God's splendor is to honor Him, which means doing what pleases Him. It means choosing Him above your friends, colleagues, and acquaintances. It means saying no to what displeases Him and holding God in high esteem.

As we have noted already, you are where you are today by God's sovereign design. Stand out to be His representative. Do your part to stand clean as a Christian and you will be surprised at how many other things begin to fall into place.

There are situations around you that will not change until you stand for God and display His splendor. You will hinder growth and spiritual blessings in other people's lives until you stand for God and do only what pleases Him.

## 2. Honor God regardless of who surrounds you.

One of the greatest reasons Christians fail to display God's splendor is the fear of who surrounds them.

Have you been in a meeting only to raise your hand and vote for what you really did not want to vote for because other people were doing it? Have you gone to places you did not want to go because your friends were headed there? Have you done some things to which you have looked with regret because you wanted to fit in?

These are examples of scenarios where those who surround us affect our choices. It is hard to display God's splendor and to stand out for Him if we cannot say no to those who surround us as we chose to honor God.

### 3. Honor God regardless of your position.

As God seeks to meet the needs of His children and people, He grooms and places believers in strategic positions. As much as it may look normal to you, understand that God is sovereign and He guides His children to specific careers. He puts a desire in your heart for a certain calling.

Knowing how God formed and wired you, you will have specific inclinations. All these, I believe, are part of His divine design. Behind your will, hard work, and aspiration is God's guiding hand to put you in certain positions for His honor and glory. Remember, it is God Who works in you, both to will and to do His good pleasure (Philippians 2:13).

Honor God wherever you are regardless of your situation. Your position of influence is God-given, and He put you in that position so you can serve His people and this nation. Display His splendor by honoring Him.

Your high position should not make you shy away from God. It should not be the reason for departing from God. Your position should not drive you from God into sin. Instead, honor God regardless of where He places you. It is He Who put you there.

### 4. Honor God regardless of your circumstances.

The Christian life can be compared to the four seasons: spring, summer, fall, and winter.

Spring brings hope and jubilance; new beginnings and growth. After a long winter, you are ready to step out and spread your wings like the beautiful butterflies. You bask in the pleasantness of the sun's warmth that brings forth exciting colors. You plant and watch everything grow. Even that which looked dead and rotten soon unfolds and puts on new foliage. This is a time of hope and anticipation. You can sing, dance, and confess together with the Psalmist, saying, "Thou, which hast shewed me great and sore troubles, shalt quicken me again, and shalt bring me up again from the depths of the earth" (Psalm 71:20).

Make this spiritual season a time for purposing to walk with God. As you reflect on all He has done for you, let your heart love Him more. Take time to get close. Seek Him. Venture into new territories of spiritual growth. Feed your soul and learn to hear God's voice as you read and memorize the Scriptures. Cultivate your walk with God. Pray and fast as you ask Him to help you die to yourself and subject your body to His will.

As the earth brings forth new growth in spring, do the same spiritually. Be proactive in loving God. Produce fruit. This is the time to allow God to prune and trim your heart. Venture into new avenues of service to God as He leads and directs. Flourish in those moments.

Summer brings joy and excitement. The brightness of the day and the longer hours of sunlight propel you into action. Summer is a time of eating new and fresh foods. Fruits and vegetables are in plenty. There is gathering of families and enjoying great times together in the sparkling rays of sunlight.

Summer is a time of joy. It is a time you forget about the winter. In reality, winter is so far removed from your mind that you don't think about its pain and sting. Like Joseph you can say, "the Lord has made me forget" (Genesis 41:51).

Spiritual summer can be equated to your mountain top experiences. This is a time when all is going well. You can feel God's presence. You trust Him and delight in His protection. Your prayers are answered, and you feel drawn to God.

Grow your worship in summer. Develop a love for praising God. Honor Him and let others know of His goodness in your life. Magnify His name.

Make it a deliberate choice to sing and extol God's name. Look at God's reminder in James 5:13b: " . . . Is any merry? let him sing psalms."

Take advantage of the jubilant moments in your life to serve God with gladness. Reach out and witness to others. Encourage God's children. Tell of His goodness.

Fall is a much-anticipated season. Temperatures begin to cool off right when you are exhausted with the scorching heat of summer. It comes at a time when the pleasures and joys of summer have left you exhausted and almost burned out.

As you look at the fields ripe for harvest, your hard work is equally camouflaged with the joys of great yields. As the trees gently shed and drop their leaves, their rare beauty brings a calmness that leads to deep reflection and ultimate thanksgiving.

Fall is a time to count your blessings as you reflect on the bountiful grace, mercy, and hope with which God filled your year. As you get into the season of thanksgiving, you, too, can confess the Word of God in Psalm 65:11 and say, "Thou crownest the year with thy goodness; and thy paths drop fatness."

Spiritual fall can be likened to those times when your life is steady. This is when you are neither climbing tough spiritual mountains nor crawling in deep valleys of despair.

Fall is a time for you to take steady steps. This is the time to feed your soul as you anchor yourself in God. This is the time to build faith before difficult times come. You will depend on the spiritual stores of fall when winter comes. Hide God's Word in your heart. You will need it in the days to come.

Make deliberate steps to walk toward God in those moments when you are basking in His blessings and provisions for you. Reflect on God's goodness and soak in His love. Remember, He is the One Who blessed and multiplied your resources. It is God Who gave the promotion, caused clients to come to your business, protected and cared for you. He provided everything you have. Without Him you are nothing. Honor and develop faith and trust. Love Him.

Winter comes with great anticipation for the blessings of Christmas as the heart is also thankful for God's grace and goodness for the entire year. Amidst the joy and gratitude is the dread for the coming cold, too.

In the dark moments of winter, the rays and the heat of the summer can only be remembered with deep longing. There is more reflection and bundling up in warm clothes, unlike the sanguine days of summer. As you look out to the dead and lifeless-looking vegetation, it takes greater effort to step out. There is limited planting or harvesting. It takes faith to trust God for spring again.

Winter is a time of deep reflection, planning, and strategizing for the new year. The main focus in winter is staying alive and warm.

What do you do in the winter seasons of life?

Honor God. Be patient when nights are long and days are dreary. Think on God's goodness and blessings in the other seasons. This will keep you hopeful.

Trust God in those dark times when you can neither see nor feel Him. Soak up His Word. Hold onto His promises and believe in His character.

Pray more. Seek Him more. Reflect and be grounded. This is the time to deepen your spiritual roots as you anchor yourself in God.

Honor God regardless of the season of life facing you spiritually. Do not compromise because of the difficulties that surround you. Display His splendor knowing that no season lasts forever.

## 5. Honor God regardless of your social status.

How many honorable individuals honor God? Can you identify prominent leaders who honor God? What about the millionaires and the billionaires of the world? How many of them reverence and think highly of God?

As we know, social status is usually associated with affluence.

I would like you to look at high social status and affluence from God's point of view. It is God Who gives you status and affluence. He does it so you can display His splendor, meet the needs of His people, and in turn bring Him honor and glory.

Look at the reason God gives in Psalm 105:44-45 for giving wealth to His beloved children.

> "And gave them the lands of the heathen: and they inherited the labour of the people; That they might observe his statutes, and keep his laws. Praise ye the Lord."

God does not trust everyone with riches and honor. He knows who can and cannot handle that. When He trusts you with the abundance of the earth and sets you in a place of affluence, honor Him.

Are you among those described in 1 Samuel 2:8 who have been greatly helped by God? "He raiseth up the poor out of the dust, and lifteth up the beggar from the dunghill, to set them among princes, and to make them inherit the throne of glory."

Has God raised you out of the dust and lifted you from the dunghill of begging? Are you in the category of these raised from utter poverty and lifted to sit among the princes and the nobles of the land? Has He given you a position of honor? Serve Him with gratitude and with a humble heart. Give Him honor and praise Him for His goodness. Serve Him with joy and gladness.

## Activities to Help You Serve This Generation in a Positive Way

Those who display God's splendor purpose to do so. Just as any project requires planning, putting in hard work, and overcoming challenges before it will succeed, so does displaying the splendor of God.

1.  Has God honored you with great associations, a position of influence, intelligence or financial stability? Use them to glorify Him and to promote His agenda in the world?

2.  In what four areas of your life must you honor God if you must display His splendor in your time?

3.  Identify three things you can do for God this year. Devote yourself to them as you ask God to use you for His honor and glory.

## Memory Verse

*But now the LORD saith, Be it far from me; for them that honour me*
*I will honour, and they that despise me shall be lightly esteemed.*

1 Samuel 2:30b

# Part Three
## Stepping Out to Display God's Splendor

*Chapter Ten*

# Unashamed to Display His Splendor

*If I could relive my life, I would devote my entire ministry*
*to reaching children for God.*

D. L. Moody[11]

## Declare God's Goodness and Faithfulness for Other Generations to See

Do not be ashamed to display God's goodness and faithfulness in your life. Don't be embarrassed to speak to others about Him either. Those who do not know God admire true Christians. They envy those whose lives are characterized with peace, trust, and hope.

You have no reason to walk folded up in knots and afraid to identify with God. It is a privilege to be associated with Him. It is an honor to be a Christian and to be counted among God's children.

There are many Christians who fear to identify themselves with God, but they need not. Know that salvation is the best gift someone can receive in this

---

11    Moody, Dwight L. *Moody's Last Sermons*. United States: Moody Publishers, 2013.

world. There are millions of people who would pay large sums of money to get the abundance of blessings that accompany salvation. Think of the many people in our world who crave peace. Think of those who cannot keep a calm mind for even ten minutes. How many endure sleepless nights because they are plagued by their conscience?

Those who do not know God yearn and desire to have what you enjoy as a child of God.

One way to display His splendor unashamedly is to depend on Him. God is faithful. Can you imagine finding someone dependable in life? What would it be like to have a friend on whom you could lean anytime? One you could trust and associate with without fear or reservations. One who looked out for your best interests every moment. A friend who encouraged and cheered you, and looked out for your health, peace, safety, and even material needs. This is just an iota of what Christ, our Savior, does for those who know Him.

It takes strength to depend on God. Contrary to what some may think and even believe, depending on God is not a sign of weakness. It is a sign of unwavering strength. Those who do not depend on Him lack the anchor of His presence. They become unstable, faithless, and fearful. Their lives are governed with much uncertainty and anxiety. They run from one place to another and try different things in the hopes of finding stability and meaning.

Those who learn to abandon themselves in the arms of God find Him a strong tower of security. He is a rock that fortresses and protects them with surety. Not only is this trust, it is faith. This is true strength.

Don't feel like you owe the world an apology for walking with God and entrusting your life to Him. Walk tall and represent Him well as you let your life be a testimony of His goodness. Exhibit His mercy. Let His love flow through you and tell of His wonders. Sing of His faithfulness, proclaim His beauty and grace and sing of His love and kindness.

Join the Psalmist in reciting and singing the words of Psalm 57:9-11 as you lift up your heart in gratitude saying, "I will praise thee, O Lord, among the people: I will sing unto thee among the nations. For thy mercy is great unto the heavens, and thy truth unto the clouds. Be thou exalted, O God, above the heavens: let thy glory be above all the earth." Walk tall and represent Him well.

When you depend on God, you display His splendor without thinking about it. It does not take effort to do it while anchored in Him. Think about a big fruit tree growing in fertile soil. Its branches do not think about producing fruit. The fruit will be a natural expectation and the branches will yield fruit abundantly by virtue of their position on the tree.

Look at how Christ explains this phenomenon in John 15:1-6:

> "I am the true vine, and my Father is the husbandman.
>
> Every branch in me that beareth not fruit he taketh away: and every branch that beareth fruit, he purgeth it, that it may bring forth more fruit.
>
> Now ye are clean through the word which I have spoken unto you.
>
> Abide in me, and I in you. As the branch cannot bear fruit of itself, except it abide in the vine; no more can ye, except ye abide in me.
>
> I am the vine, ye are the branches: He that abideth in me, and I in him, the same bringeth forth much fruit: for without me ye can do nothing."

The secret to displaying His splendor is to abide in Him. When you do it, God's spiritual laws will ensure you are displaying it. Subsequently, your own life will be loaded with spiritual fruit. You will not need to tell anyone that you are displaying His splendor. It will be evident to those who see and interact with you.

As you can see, it all starts when you purpose to trust God. You display His splendor when you decide to follow and to be associated with Him.

How else do you display God's splendor unashamedly?

Use your position of influence to further the kingdom of God. Think of how your good standing can affect God's kingdom ten, twenty, thirty years down the road. What can you do at the moment to ensure that God is served, revered, and honored in the coming years?

What is the one thing we do when we want more returns in the future for what we have at the moment? We invest. If you want your money to grow and to give you good dividends in the future, you must invest. Without investing, you may use it up and have nothing for the future. The same is true with spiritual work. For you to see God's work grow and produce good fruit in the future, you must invest. Of course, we do not take our works and fruit to the bank but we can apply this principle in different aspects of our serving God.

How do you invest in the future of God's work? One smart way to do it is to invest in young people. You do this by placing the torch of the gospel in their hands as you nurture and groom them to maturity.

You do it by equipping them. You prayerfully look ahead to determine their future needs for God's work. You step out in faith to follow God and to do what will benefit His kingdom.

## Get Practical

It is hard to display God's splendor when you are not genuine or when you cannot step out to do what God desires. One way to get practical is to make every day count for eternity. Purpose to serve God and to invest in eternity every single day. Just as you map or plan your work and time, make a deliberate effort to include spiritual services.

Think of practical ways to encourage and grow people. Pray and seek opportunities to plant spiritual seeds. Water and nurture them to maturity.

A good way to do this is to reflect on your life at the moment. Closely look at the past seven days and identify the opportunities you missed to display God's splendor. Think of those you would have witnessed to but did not. Think of how many you would have visited, written to, and encouraged. What about those who needed your prayers? Do you know people with different needs you would have helped? Did God put certain assignments on your heart? Did He ask you to do something you did not do?

Today is a brand-new opportunity to hear, follow, and display God's splendor. Seize the moment. Go all out for God. Do as He directs. Seek Him. Hear Him. Obey Him. Do what will positively influence people today and in the future.

## An Influence for Our Generation

Use your high position of honor to influence the youth and those who will carry the work of God into the future.

How do you do that?

There are many ways to invest in people to advance the kingdom of God and to display His splendor wherever they are. Here are just a few ideas to help you catch the vision and get started.

### 1. Become a mentor, a coach, an advisor, a teacher, or a counselor.

Become a coach? A counselor? "What do I talk about?" you may ask. Talk about what we are dealing with right now—the emotional, social, physical and economic struggles. Many Christians desire to be involved in things that yield eternal dividends, but they do not know how to do it. Most Christians will devote their time and money if the course for which they are devoted will lead to eternal rewards, whether for themselves or for another.

This is a good starting point. Teach them sound doctrine regarding what the Bible says about the future of both believers and non-believers. Let them see the future reality that faces their relatives who do not know God.

Teach them how to evangelize. Train them. Have lessons on how to witness to sinners about God's love for them. Go through Scriptures for them to use in witnessing. Create opportunities for them to practice on one another. This will give them confidence as they familiarize themselves with what God's Word says about salvation. Take them out on practical sessions. Choose an evening or a Saturday and set it aside for witnessing. Pair up or team up in small groups and talk to people about God. A trio works well. One person can be the spokesperson, and one can help in finding relevant Scriptures as the other engages in continuous silent prayer and maintain the spiritual vigil.

Do your homework before you engage in evangelism. Identify the community you desire to evangelize. Strategize how many homes or people you will target. Understand where those people will be at the time of your arrival. You do not want to get to empty homes or places. Know whom you expect to find in those areas. Are they homes or is it street evangelism with a certain type of people only. This is important in helping you know how to prepare your team.

## 2. Form Bible study groups.

Start a small Bible study group. Teach sound doctrine. Teach them how to live for God and how to be positive influences in a dark world. Focus their attention on what is eternal and how to invest in the kingdom of God. Teach them the practical principles of Christian living.

Shift their focus from a self-defeating and self-destroying entertainment mindset to focus on spiritual growth and eternal investment. Draw them from self-centeredness. Instead, teach them to listen to God and to follow Him in obedience and reaching out to those around them. Create opportunities for them to practice what they learn.

## 3. Form prayer groups.

Imagine meeting to pray before going out to evangelize and witness the birth of many souls joining the kingdom of God. Such practical results ignite a spiritual fire and change the hearts of believers. They create an inner hunger and a desire for spiritual growth. Imagine praying for Sunday services and witnessing God's powerful move as He speaks and meets the spiritual needs of those assembled. This will make your group want to pray more. Prayer will take a different form, as they trust God for specific results. This is a foundation for spiritual growth.

Like evangelism, let prayer sessions be orderly and profitable. Let those who come to pray know the order for the session. Have the main prayer issues of the day ready. Fill in with other needs from your group and guide them to pray intentionally for each item with commitment.

Point your group to pray for the spiritual needs of different people groups. Engage them in praying for the nation and the community. Let them bear the burden of what it will take to see spiritual change in the community. Let them see their role in meeting the spiritual needs in their families, church, communities, nation, and even the world. This is how you avail yourself to be a vessel to display God's splendor.

### 4. Involve your group in acts of service.

Identify projects on which they can work and even give their time and money. Engage them in providing shelter for the homeless and those who live in tattered habitats. Seek opportunities for your group to assist in distributing relief food. Let them be part of teams that bring hope and healing to communities devastated by natural disasters.

Encourage them to emulate the Lord Jesus Christ and to be servants. Let them serve in homeless shelters, children's homes, orphanages, and in underprivileged communities. As the Prophet Jeremiah correctly noted in Lamentation 3:51, our eyes affect our hearts. Opening people's eyes to the needs of others has a way of reaching to the heart and changing lives for good. It is from seeing others' need for help that God touches the hearts of His people and in turn calls them to His service to meet those specific needs.

Seek opportunities for your group to go on mission trips in carefully selected places. Let them pray for the mission devotedly and watch God do His work in the lives of His people.

## 5. Organize or send your group to spiritual camps, retreats, or conferences.

Identify local churches and/or organizations that conduct good spiritual activities and involve your group. Let these be intentional opportunities for their growth. Let them be moments for tenderizing their hearts to the working of God and His calling in their lives. Organize them in a way that they will offer opportunities to sensitize their hearts to the needs that surround them.

Teach them how to identify and meet needs as they partner with God in ministering to humanity.

## 6. Encourage your group to aspire to serve God.

One of the best things you can do for young people, or any Christian, is to direct their focus on God. Exhort them to meet for prayer. This can be in homes and in smaller groups.

Inspire them to be witnesses for Christ our Savior. Fuel their spiritual fire and let them be sold out for Christ. Let them look for positions and places where they can serve God wholeheartedly.

Disciple them to take up the baton and run for God. Let them take responsibility for the spreading of the gospel and for doing God's work.

### Be Deliberate with Your Position

Remember, God has put you where you are and given you a position of influence for a reason. He wants you to use it for His honor and glory. You must be deliberate in order to display His splendor and do the works for which He created you. It is easy to miss your daily opportunities. It is easy to slack off, and even become careless.

Step out and be deliberate about your desires, your plans, and your actions. Begin by surrounding yourself with godly friends. Find those who are unashamed to belong to God. Those may be people at your workplace, on the executive team, in your prayer group, in your association, community, or school. Do not just choose anybody. Let this be a team of friends with whom you can pray, study, and discuss the deep things of God.

Organize for meetings where you can pray, plan, and implement strategies to grow the kingdom of God. Begin with your Jerusalem—your most proximal area of operation. Christ was intentional as He commissioned the disciples into His work. Follow his example. First, He told them to go and teach all nations. He told them what to teach and the reason for teaching. He also assured the beloved group that He would be with them every step of the way. See Matthew 28:19-20:

> "Go ye therefore, and teach all nations, baptizing them in the name of the Father, and of the Son, and of the Holy Ghost: Teaching them to observe all things whatsoever I have commanded you: and, lo, I am with you always, even unto the end of the world. Amen."

Now look at how the disciples reached the nations as God prepared them to step out into the great commission. Christ would empower them in the work for which they were called. But look at the order as stated in Acts 1:8:

> "But ye shall receive power, after that the Holy Ghost is come upon you: and ye shall be witnesses unto me both in Jerusalem, and in all Judaea, and in Samaria, and unto the uttermost part of the earth."

The promise was made right there in Jerusalem. The disciples waited in that spiritually monumental city until God endowed them with power to do His work (Acts 1:4).

There was no way the disciples would risk everything by going to other nations before evangelizing right where they were. It was from Jerusalem that they would move to the surrounding area—Judea, then Samaria, and finally to the ends of the world.

Emulate this example and start by looking at the spiritual needs within your immediate area. What are they? How can you meet them? What will it take to do the work effectively and efficiently? How should you involve your team? What roles should every member play? When can you do it and when should you start?

God honors godly visions that aim to promote His work. He will stand with you to encourage, to empower, and to give you what you need to do His work. Do not be afraid to begin small. Remember, most people stand on the sidelines until something picks up momentum and shows signs of success before they join. Let this not discourage you. Know that the majority of Christians delight in collaborating on projects that have eternal rewards. Besides, God Who calls you is faithful. He will give you the right team of people to propel your vision. Do not forget that He is with you. He will neither leave nor forsake you.

If you do not pick up the vision to meet the spiritual needs of your greatest area of influence, spiritual darkness will prevail. The light of God will grow dim. People will shy from talking and associating with God. They will silence the voice of God and many will miss an opportunity for eternal life. Remember, where there is no vision, people perish (Proverbs 29:18).

## Make Good Use of Your Position

Use your position to be a good ambassador for Christ. Credit God with your success. Those who surround you should see your honor, love, and reverence for God as they witness the joy and peace that come from Him. Let them taste of His goodness through the honesty, integrity, kindness, efficiency and humility that permeate your life as they see your genuine interest in their welfare. Give them a reason to be attracted to your God. Let them know it is cool to serve God regardless of who you are, where you are, and the position you hold.

Imagine the great impact the Prophet Daniel had in Babylon as He worked with his team of godly friends. Daniel did not waver in his love for God, nor did he compromise because he was in a foreign land. He did not falter or water down his love when he ascended to a position of honor as a government official advising the king. Together with Meshach, Shadrach, and Abednego, he sought God and lived above reproach. Many high-ranking officials in the Babylonian government envied and hated Daniel but also knew of his love for God.

Those days of Babylon with Daniel, Meshach, Shadrach, and Abednego are long gone. We cannot bring those fine Hebrew boys to influence our day. God has you and me in the right place to step into their shoes and stand for Him. He has put you right where you should display His glory and splendor. Get ready to work. Put muscles to the plow and do a great work for God. It is your turn to influence men and women for God. Take the opportunity and be a good witness for Christ. Let your light shine. Point someone to eternity.

### Activities to Help You Build Courage to Serve God as He Desires

God has put you where you are and given you a position of influence for a reason. He wants you to use it for His honor and glory. You must be deliberate in order to display God's splendor and do the works for which He has created you. It is easy to miss your daily opportunities. It is easy to slack off and even be careless.

1. What makes you afraid or ashamed to stand out for God and to serve Him as you display His splendor?

2. How can you use your position regardless of who you are to make positive influence on those around you and in the kingdom of God?

3. In what ways can you invest in the future of God's work?

4. Find five young people to mentor. Devote your time, effort, energy and relevant resources to see them grow into mature servants of God who will in turn influence this world for God.

## Memory Verses

*Thou therefore, my son, be strong in the grace that is in Christ Jesus. And the things that thou hast heard of me among many witnesses, the same commit thou to faithful men, who shall be able to teach others also.*

2 Timothy 2:1-2

## Chapter Eleven

# Resisting Temptation

*A holy life will produce the deepest impression.*
*Lighthouses blow no horns; they only shine.*

D. L. Moody[12]

### Learning to Resist Temptation

If we desire to display God's splendor and to be a positive influence in our world today, by the help of the Spirit, we must work on the art of resisting temptation.

As every believer knows, it is not easy to resist temptation. Resisting is not something we do once and attain mastery. Resisting temptation is something we work on daily. Sometimes we fail and other times succeed. There are days when we fail miserably, but there other days when we are able to resist and stand our ground. The more we commit to mastering and resisting temptation, the more we will have victory and delight in growing closer to God.

The devil's strategy has not changed since the days of Adam and Eve. Just as he disrupted the ecclesiastical relationship that existed between God and the first couple, he does the same today. Satan understands that the easiest

12   Moody, Dwight L. *Moody's Last Sermons*. United States: Moody Publishers, 2013.

way to get you off course is to drive a wedge between you and God. He works to draw you from God, and enjoys seeing your conscience plagued with guilt and shame. That way, he keeps you afraid of approaching God or enjoying fellowship with Him.

Satan's tool of choice is temptation. He lures and deceives, hoping to see you act contrary to God's commands. He understands that God hates sin. Sin causes God to turn a deaf ear to those in habitual rebellion. He disregards their prayers (Deuteronomy 1:45; Psalm 66:18). This can discourage Christians.

Have you tried talking to someone who did not care to listen to you? How did you feel? Does your heart beat with a desire to continue speaking? Do you look forward to talking to them again when they ignore you repeatedly? No. This discourages your heart. It makes you stay to yourself. You avoid that individual. This is what happens to us when we indulge and let our sins characterize our lives. Our unrepented transgressions keep God silent. That is what Satan longs to see. That is why sin is one of the greatest reasons for our inability to display God's splendor.

Before we can resist temptation successfully, we must understand the process of temptation. Let us look at this together as we walk towards displaying God's splendor.

## 1. Understand that Satan is a schemer

Satan can throw temptations in our path on a whim, but this is not his usual tactic. He strategizes and schemes, studying to understand how best to tempt us and find the most effective ways to bring us down. He will focus on our likes and dislikes as he observes patterns in order to formulate and execute his plans.

We must understand that Satan is smart. He will not bring what he knows we can resist easily. He will purposely set up traps with our weaknesses in mind and learn what might make us stumble. He works to understand what will cause our hearts to run away from God.

## 2. There are opportune moments for temptation

Imagine a friend offering you a sweater in the heat of the summer. Now imagine that same offer coming to you on a cold morning while awaiting to change a car tire on the side of the road. When are you likely to take the offer? When will it be easy to resist the sweater?

Our adversary the devil looks for the opportune time to throw his well-cultivated baits of temptation at us. He waits for a time when we are vulnerable and seemingly in need.

Satan will not tempt someone to get into a secret, promiscuous relationship while they are enjoying spiritual growth and intimacy with their spouse. He knows that person will reason it out, and their spirit, which is sensitive to God, will send off clear warning signals of danger.

When does he tempt men and women with thoughts of unfaithfulness? Usually when:

- There is a strain in their relationship
- When there is dissatisfaction
- Searching for something more
- Away from home
- Fighting bad feelings against their spouse
- There are misunderstandings
- There is fighting, resentment, and rejection
- There is a lure and a deception for something good

Look at how this scheme was used against Joseph.

Joseph left his home in obedience to his father's commission to go and check on his brothers who were tending the family flocks. You can almost see the young man skipping, jumping, whistling, and playing along while on his journey from Hebron to the fields toward Shechem (Genesis 37:13-14).

Why is Joseph singing and having a great time on this journey?

It is because Joseph is special. Look at where all his brothers are as he hangs around his father. They are enduring the heat of the day, looking after the family animals while Joseph is enjoying favors and special treatment at home. The Bible tells us why Joseph was special.

"Israel loved Joseph more than all his children, because he was the son of his old age: and he made him a coat of many colours" (Genesis 37:3).

At this time, Joseph is not too young to be with his brothers. If he is old enough to take the long journey all by himself on foot, he can take care of the family treasures, too. As a matter of fact, the Bible reveals that Joseph was seventeen years old (Genesis 37:2).

Not only was Joseph a beloved son in the home, he was heralded. This was a young man who had unusual dreams. His dreams were unique and significant. They pointed to a future of leadership and prosperity. They denoted God's hand of blessing and honor on his life.

At that time, God spoke to His people through angels and dreams— dreams that were significant and carried special messages were well known by the people. Joseph was in that beloved category of those whom the hand of Yahweh would favor and prosper. Both his parents and brothers knew and believed him, but his brothers envied him.

Joseph arrived at Shechem but did not get his brothers. A stranger saw Joseph wandering in the field, and on learning that Joseph was searching for his brothers, he directed Joseph to Dothan (Genesis 37:15-17).

Joyfully, and without a complaint, Joseph trekked another ten miles to see his brothers. After all, when all is going well and your heart is charmed by the prospects of a glorious and beautiful future, such walks can be pleasant and delightful.

Joseph did not anticipate what awaited him in Dothan. His brothers' jealousy swelled into hate as they seized the opportunity to act while he was away from his beloved parents. They stripped Joseph of the wonderful and colorful coat and threw him into a cistern. The young men's hearts were vicious and cruel. They were ready to watch their brother die. After all, they were away from home and far away from accountability.

"Here comes the dreamer," they said. "Come now therefore, and let us slay him, and cast him into some pit, and we will say, Some evil beast hath devoured him: and we shall see what will become of his dreams" (Genesis 37:20).

Look at the temptation of malice, hate, and sinister motives when the heart believes that no one is watching and no one will know. These are moments when the heart will be tempted to slander someone. It will seize an opportunity for revenge. We will do it not because that person is bad but because they are better than us. Our hearts will do it because, like Joseph's brothers, we want to put an end to their success. We will do it because we do not want them to ascend to that position of favor and honor.

## How Does the Heart Do It?

We speak evil of the person even when we know we are wrong. We lie and formulate exaggerated stories against them. We write malicious information and seek audience with their leader behind closed doors.

Look at what took place as Joseph lay in a cistern awaiting death, and later as he journeyed to Egypt.

Joseph's brothers sat down to eat. I have always thought to myself that it must have been Joseph who brought that very food to them. How cold can the heart be to sit down and eat while your brother is struggling for his life? Nevertheless, when the heart yields to temptation, there is no telling how far it can go. One can run many miles while on their sinful mission and engage in any number of alarming activities.

Joseph's brothers later changed their minds. They got the boy out of the well and sold him to Ishmaelites who took Joseph to Egypt (Genesis 37:25-28).

As it is with most temptations, after the act, there is a camouflage. Joseph's brothers had to face their father and come up with a plan to cover their plot.

They took Joseph's coat, killed a goat, and dipped the coat in the blood. They carried Joseph's coat of many colors to their father and said, "this have we found: know now whether it be thy son's coat or no" (Genesis 37:31-32).

The day was not over for the wicked schemers.

Jacob recognized the coat as his beloved son's. As plotted, he fell for the scheme that a wild beast had devoured Joseph. The old man tore his clothes, put on sack clothes, and mourned for his son many days. As he lamented and grieved, the same plotters comforted him as they sealed their wicked deal.

The human heart is capable of wicked schemes and Satan capitalizes on that. He knows how to tempt. He knows how to ignite passions and fires that are not easy to extinguish. He knows which cords to touch in your life in order to accomplish his evil plans. This is why it is important to understand temptations.

### 3. Temptations come to all Christians: those walking closely to God and those who walk afar off.

There are many Christians who believe the myth that temptations do not come to those who walk closely to God. Satan enjoys that. He likes it when we believe a lie. This way he can deploy his plans and catch Christians off guard. Such a belief leaves Christians in a strained relationship with God. This is because they view temptations as an indication that God has forsaken them. This makes them prayerless and keeps them from God. Nothing pleases Satan more than disrupting communication lines between God and His children. That is his entire mission for temptation.

Joseph was not exempt from temptations even in those difficult times.

The Ishmaelites sold Joseph to the Midianites. The Midianites sold him in Egypt to Potiphar, an officer of Pharaoh who was a captain of the guard. From his close shave of death in the cistern, Joseph became a slave in Egypt.

Again, Satan seized an opportunity. Joseph got to work in the house of his master in Egypt. The God Who had given Joseph dreams in Canaan still favored the young man. He caused Joseph to prosper in everything he did. Joseph was beloved by Potiphar and it was evident to his master that the hand of God was with Joseph. Potiphar put Joseph in charge of his household and entrusted everything he owned to the young man's care.

While Potiphar saw the majesty of God in Joseph, his wife's eyes focused on something different. While Potiphar acknowledged the favor and presence of God abiding with Joseph, his wife was attracted to the extraordinary young man in her house. God's hand of blessing on Joseph did not stop the tempted woman from making seductive advances.

"Lie with me," she said.

Can you imagine the shock that must have struck Joseph as he watched her and heard those words?

What did she lack? What did she want? After all, she was among the nobles of Egypt who were reverenced and served on a daily basis. She must have been the envy of multitudes of women. If it is glamor and fame, she had it.

In those ancient times, not many could rise to the position of her husband. The man must have had outstanding leadership qualities. His personality, demeanor, and education had to measure up to the position. His decorum must have been majestic, too. How many women would have longed to have such a man in that nation? How many would have lived in utter submission and gratitude for attaining the favor of such a man? However, her heart was not satisfied.

Our adversary uses such unsatisfied hearts to pose dangerous temptations to the children of God. He knows how to get to our hearts. He knows the lure that can make us fall with ease. None of us is too spiritual to be tempted.

### Activities to Help You Display the Splendor of God

Satan's tool of choice against God's people is temptation. He lures and deceives, hoping to see you act contrary to God's commands. He understands that God hates sin.

1.  Identify the weak areas in your life that Satan may use to fight you and to distract your service to God.
2.  Commit each area identified to God in prayer and ask for His help.

3. Take practical steps to strengthen and work on each area as you resist the enemy from invading and striking.

4. Identify four people who have the same weaknesses. Work together to pray, encourage one another, and to formulate strategies for standing against the enemy in your lives.

## Memory Verses

*Blessed is the man that endureth temptation: for when he is tried, he shall receive the crown of life, which the Lord hath promised to them that love him.*

*Let no man say when he is tempted, I am tempted of God: for God cannot be tempted with evil, neither tempteth he any man:*

*But every man is tempted, when he is drawn away of his own lust, and enticed.*

*Then when lust hath conceived, it bringeth forth sin: and sin, when it is finished, bringeth forth death.*

James 1:12-15

## Chapter Twelve

# Standing Your Ground and Acting

*Every instance of obedience, from right motives, strengthens us spiritually,*
*whilst every act of disobedience weakens us.*

George Muller[13]

### Temptations Demand Decisions and Actions

Joseph did not keep quiet. He replied to Potiphar's wife saying,

> "Behold, my master wotteth not what is with me in the house, and he hath committed all that he hath to my hand; There is none greater in this house than I; neither hath he kept back any thing from me but thee, because thou art his wife: how then can I do this great wickedness, and sin against God?" (Genesis 39:8-9).

Joseph's heart remained fixed on God.

I do not think this was the first time Joseph was making up his mind to honor God in a tough situation. I can imagine Joseph imploring God to save his life while he lay in the cistern back home.

---

13    Muller, George. *The Autobiography of George Muller*. N.p.: Whitaker House, 1996.

What a joy and relief it must have brought to Joseph's heart when his brothers finally pulled him out of the well. Imagine the prayers he must have made in that dark hole. Imagine the promises he must have made to Yahweh, the giver of his dreams, as his heart longed for him in desperation.

I do not think that was the last time Joseph besought God wholeheartedly either.

Imagine what went on in Joseph's heart as his brothers negotiated his wages with the Midianites before settling on twenty pieces of silver. Imagine the prayers he made at his wits end as he pleaded with his brothers in vain.

What did he tell God as he journeyed to a far land as a slave? Did he follow quietly, awaiting his fate? Did he ask God for favor? Did he ask Yahweh to put him in a favorable place? You see, there was no guarantee where a slave could find himself. Only one thing mattered to the one who sold slaves. All he looked for was a good price. On the other hand, the buyer of slaves cared only for what kind of laborers his money bought.

Nothing could stop Joseph from being grateful. What an honor to be placed in Potiphar's house. As though that was not enough, his master trusted him. He put everything under Joseph's care. This meant that Joseph had a voice. He had a say in what went on in that house. Joseph was not subjected to the hard labor that most slaves faced. This also meant that Joseph was not mistreated. He had good food, good clothes, and a good place to sleep quietly and peacefully.

Joseph must have committed his whole heart to God. Imagine how he must have thanked the God of his fathers. I can imagine Joseph submitting to God and purposing to reverence Him in life. Right there in Potiphar's house, Joseph must have resolved to love, obey, and follow Yahweh's commandments as his way of saying thank you.

Such unwavering faith and truth in God did not deter the steps of the woman whose heart was set on her young prey.

She pestered Joseph day after day to sleep with her.

Joseph neither consented nor stayed near her.

Satan is relentless in his attempts to trap the children of God. Saying no today does not stop him from striking or trying again tomorrow. In fact, when you resist him today, he looks for better opportunities to present his temptation. He coats temptation with pleasantries and packages it in enticing ways to make you succumb.

God rightly describes Satan as an adversary who walks around as a lion seeking whom to devour (1 Peter 5:8). That is why our heavenly Father warns all His children to be sober and to be vigilant.

### Temptations Demand That You Stand Your Ground

Satan hurled a spiritual grenade at Joseph.

> "And it came to pass about this time, that Joseph went into the house to do his business; and there was none of the men of the house there within. And she caught him by his garment, saying, Lie with me: and he left his garment in her hand, and fled, and got him out" (Genesis 39:11-12).

Look at the intersection of opportunity with temptation.

This is the most dangerous part of any temptation, where many Christians stumble. It is easy to resist a temptation when the opportunity is missing. It is also easy to look at opportune moments with a different eye when temptation is not knocking on your door.

What do you do when you are alone, far from anyone who knows you, and you are approached by the person who so desires you? Mark you—this is no ordinary person. This is a celebrity; someone well-known and respected.

How do you say no to a person who determines what you eat, drink, or what you could have and fail to have? How do you say no to the authority figure in your life for the sake of God? How do you resist the offer when whoever is offering it can keep it silent to the grave? How do you say No to the person who has a hand on the power switch that determines whether you will live or die that day?  How do you resist such temptation when you are young and single with hot blood constantly running through your veins?

Joseph resisted the temptation and ran, while Potiphar's wife remained with his coat.

This is a good time to understand important concepts about temptations.

As we live and combat temptations, let us look at how temptations unfold and grow.

### 1. Satan is still at work.

While Joseph lived long ago, Satan is still present and at work. He does not want you to sing the praises of God or display His splendor.

Satan wants you to live defeated. He rejoices when any Christian falls to one of his temptations. He knows how to crush you and hold you captive. He knows how hard it is for you to love and serve God while in a constant and recurring cycle of failure. As long as he can keep you preoccupied with temptations, he knows your focus will be removed from advancing the kingdom of God.

### 2. Every Christian faces temptation.

Those who learn to resist and stand against the whispers and schemes of Satan join Joseph's company. They display God's splendor regardless of what faces them.

Those who resist temptations are not superhumans. They are feeble individuals whose hearts beat with a deep desire to please God and to stand for His cause. God gives them strength to withstand temptations.

Those who resist temptations stay vigilant. They are watchful in prayer because that is the only way to maintain spiritual alertness against an enemy who is so subtle and disguised. They acknowledge their vulnerability. They understand how easy it is to fall. Nevertheless, they also acknowledge and embrace the God they serve Who has power to help them fight against the enemy and win. Those who stand lean on God. This is because there is no other pillar on which to lean if they must overcome temptation. It is only because of God that they can stand.

Think about it for a moment. Even Jesus, the only Son of God, Who is God Himself, was tempted (Matthew 4). This leaves no chance for anyone. Every Christian will be tempted. Those who will conger temptations must embrace and depend on the strength God gives.

## 3. Learn to say no.

Not many people learn to say no and to stand with it. Satan knows how to manipulate your conscience and to play around with guilt. He knows how hard it is to say no and how easy it is to say yes and follow along.

## The Process of Temptation

Psalm 1 admonishes readers to not yield to temptation: "Blessed is the man that walketh not in the counsel of the ungodly, nor standeth in the way of sinners, nor sitteth in the seat of the scornful."

Yielding to temptation begins in subtle ways that may not be obvious even to the one who is tempted. Satan manipulates you in this fashion, to keep you blind to his presence so you may not identify him and resist the temptation.

You move from walking, to standing, to sitting.

A. Once a Christian is caught up in the company of people who do not know God, he or she must know that temptations will increase and resisting them will become more difficult.

Joining this new group will be exciting at first. There will be a temporary glow and flow of energy as your feet set on the evil adventure. However, for the Christian, this stage will be filled with warning signals of love. God will make it clear that His child is stepping into foul and dangerous waters. How will God do this?

- God will give caution. He gave us the Holy Spirit as a witness on the inside to hold us back. He will prick our conscience to know that it is wrong.
- God will use His Word to point us back to Himself and to speak to our specific situations. As we open our Bibles God will direct us to Scriptures that address our hearts. They will jump out at us and make our hearts leap with holy fear.
- God will use other people to let us know if we are on the wrong track. God has a way of guiding and directing conversations to the exact point of need. God will send people with words of caution. Those who love us and pray for us will be the first to caution us out of deep love. Listen to them.
- God will use His servants. He will send His timely Word through the preaching of His Word. Remember, it is God Who appoints pastors, evangelists, and teachers to His work. He will give them what benefits His children, the hearers.

So, do not be surprised to attend a church service only to hear the preacher and the teacher talk straight to your heart. They are God's messengers of good news to rescue us from the jaws of Satan. This is a good point to make an about-turn and save your soul from endless sorrows. Those who do not listen move on to the second description of the Psalms—they stand to commune with sinners and sit down with scorners.

B. You will move from merely associating with them to standing and talking with them. This means that you chose to belong and to be part of who they are.

- This means that your heart and mind embrace the members and the activities of the group. You enjoy time with your new team. This indicates that you are initiated into the group.

- You listen to what they say and agree with them. You make and execute plans together. You take advice from them and act on it as your own.
- This is the point where Satan feeds you with his lies. He blinds you to the truth of God. It is while standing, watching, listening, and soaking it in that he makes you start questioning the truth. You debate with God's Word in your heart and mind as you seek to justify what you want to do.
- It is while standing and soaking it in that you fight your conscience.
- The initial stages of this phase are characterized by hiding. You straddle the fence, desiring to join the new wicked group yet at the same time not wanting those who are godly to associate you with it. You rationalize everything in order to sooth your conscience. You fight God as He pursues you, and you resist those who tell you the truth. Hate and resentment begin to develop in your heart as you slowly walk away from God's precepts. You disregard advice and fight against what you have learned. The desire to belong makes your heart long to act and engage in activities that displease God.

C. The last thing that seals your departure from God and plunges you into a group that will lead you into wickedness is sitting with those who scoff or mock.

- This means you have a place in the group. At this point, not only are you accepted but also you have a place of prominence, honor, and even leadership. You have a say in what happens in the group. You are a policy maker and an implementer.
- One thing that Satan does at this moment is point out peoples' mistakes before you. Those who loved and cared for you become your enemies. You resent those who tell you the truth. Instead,

you believe lies from the members of your new group. You will count them to be your only true friends and cling to them as though you never had better friends.

- Understand that all this is a process. It is masterminded by the enemy. Satan will work on your newfound friends, too. They will help you see and dwell on the mistakes of those who truly love you but appear to be standing in your way.

- You refuse to take responsibility, instead you blame everyone else. You will find reasons to accuse them for anything and everything. You will accuse them of neglect. You will blame them for never giving you a chance. Your heart will get to a point where it will believe all these lies to be true. Unfortunately, because you are under the influence of Satan, you will act on each one of them until God reaches out to you and brings you back to Himself.

- You will mock, hate, and make a laughingstock of those who truly love you. Believing a lie causes you to profane God.

- Because you will want to show your new group how much you appreciate them, you will take a seat with what I call wicked dignity. You take your position for all to recognize and acknowledge. You increase in arrogance. You will spearhead activities that will cause members of that same group to laugh and mock at God as Satan rejoices at his victory. Surprisingly, you will not see or understand the mockery. Instead, you will move deeper into indulges that will shutter your soul. Your heart will be cold to God and you will surprise yourself to see how far you can walk away from those who truly love you.

## Activities to Help You Stand Your Ground and Act

Satan is relentless in his attempts to trap the children of God. Your saying no today does not stop him from striking or trying again tomorrow. In fact, when you resist him today, he looks for better opportunities to present his temptation. He coats the temptation with pleasantries and packages it in enticing ways to make you succumb.

1. To whom must you say no if you were to display the splendor of God in your life?

2. To what must you say no in order to display God's splendor and to be a lighthouse in your days?

3. Identify four people from whom you must distance yourself in order to fulfill the purposes of God in your life.

4. As you get serious with God, it is also necessary to get honest. Have you wronged people in your life? Have your actions been hurtful and damaging? Ask God for forgiveness.

5. Take another necessary step towards your healing and become a displayer of God's splendor. Approach the individuals you have wronged and hurt and ask for their forgiveness.

## Memory Verse

*Blessed is the man that walketh not in the counsel of the ungodly,*
*nor standeth in the way of sinners, nor sitteth in the seat of the scornful.*

Psalm 1:1

## Chapter Thirteen

# Making Deliberate Choices to Serve Better

*If I take care of my character, my reputation will take care of me.*

D. L. Moody[14]

### Dealing with Temptation

How do you resist temptation? How easy is it to resist temptation? Are there Christians who actually resist temptation? Do they succeed? When faced with temptations, how can Christians overcome them?

If you find yourself asking any of the above questions, it means that you are genuine and practical. Not only are temptations real but they are tough to resist. However, there is even a greater truth: you resist temptations more than you realize.

Think about it for a moment.

You chose to get out of bed today. This means you resisted the temptation to sleep all day. You got dressed and went about your duties. This also means that you resisted idleness. You went to the store over the weekend and bought

---

14   Moody, Dwight L. *Moody's Last Sermons*. United States: Moody Publishers, 2013.

items for use. Evidently, you resisted impulse buying and the compulsions to buy too much. Your paying for the items bought is a good indication that you did not shoplift. When you take time to study, you resist failure. When you work hard on your farm and projects, you resist laziness.

As you can see, within you is an in-built ability to make choices. You have the power to say either yes or no. This phenomenon comes into play while dealing with temptations.

Temptations present themselves as choices we must make: should I do it or should I not? Should I go or should I not? Should I say yes, or should I refuse and say no? Should I take it or should I not? Think about the temptations you face and see whether they fit this description or not.

Every day, you make choices regarding what to touch. You decide what to see and what not to see. You make up your mind on what to put in your body. You make choices for your feet, your ears, your mouth, and body as a whole.

These choices influence your days and determine your productivity. The choices you make regarding temptations also determine the quality of your Christian life. A constant cycle of falling to temptation leaves you spiritually empty, tired, and malnourished. That is why you must master resisting temptation.

## Facing Temptations with a Sober Eye

Let us look at practical steps to resisting temptation.

As we go through these steps together, I would like you to think of real life situations and make practical applications. Imagine you have an enemy who is making plans to attack you. Somehow, you catch wind of the plot and the details of when he will come and by whom he will be accompanied. What do you do? Do you sit still in panic and wait for the attack or do you take it to be a hoax and not prepare at all?

If you are like most people I know, I am sure you will prepare for the attack. How can you prepare? You can do several things depending on where you are and what is available.

1.  You make sure you are awake and not sleeping when the enemy comes.

2.  You are alert. You might rely on coffee, but I can assure you your adrenaline will keep you moving.

3.  You prepare to counter the attack. How do you this?

You may inform and invite the police to safeguard your house and compound that day as well as look at the entry points to your home to put secure measures in place. Barricading and reinforcing weaker areas to the house will not be an option. You will get valiant men to help you fight back.

I am sure you will get weapons with which to fight. You will formulate a plan and rehearse what you must do on the day of. Moreover, who knows, you might practice skills and moves to fight back and defeat the enemy. I know you will do something.

There is one last thing you may decide to do depending on your enemy. It may be wise to run away. How will you face a fierce enemy if you do not have the right weapons or when you are unprepared?

These are practical ways to face an enemy here in our physical world. Surprisingly, these same strategies work with spiritual enemies. There are good measures to take while dealing with temptations.

How?

Let us look at them.

## 1. Know your weaknesses

Most enemies will attack your weak area. The enemy will delight in getting to your blind and weak side. Satan does the same. You must know your weaknesses if you intend to win spiritual battles. Knowing your weakness will put your feet on a path of safety and reinforcement.

To be blind and oblivious to your weaknesses is to sit and do nothing when you know your enemy is coming. Satan likes assumptions. He enjoys working with Christians whose egos are so enlarged that they cannot prepare for spiritual attacks. This is because Satan is an enemy who watches his prey before he launches his attacks. He knows you more than you may know or understand. He studies your likes and dislikes. He takes time to understand what will bring you down.

When Satan pursued Samson, he focused on the prophet's weakness: women. Satan knew that though Samson was a powerful man filled with the Spirit of God and destined for great things, he could not resist women. That is what he used to bring him down.

Look at what crushed Solomon, the wisest man on earth. It was the same weakness. Solomon loved women. God's description of Solomon in 1 Kings 11:1 is not a good commentary for a king and a man chosen for the purposes of God:

> "But king Solomon loved many strange women, together with the daughter of Pharaoh, women of the Moabites, Ammonites, Edomites, Zidonians, and Hittites."

The enemy uses what you love and enjoy to bring you down. In fact, when he offers it to you, you will not realize it is bait. It will look like a treat, a favor, or a cordial act. However, while your heart enjoys it, the enemy will strike with all his force. He wants to make maximum use of the opportunity before your eyes open to his schemes.

Look at what happened to Solomon, a man beloved of God and chosen to build a dwelling place for the Most High God and a sanctuary for His people:

> "For it came to pass, when Solomon was old, that his wives turned away his heart after other gods: and his heart was not perfect with the Lord his God, as was the heart of David his father.
>
> For Solomon went after Ashtoreth the goddess of the Zidonians, and after Milcom the abomination of the Ammonites.
>
> And Solomon did evil in the sight of the Lord, and went not fully after the Lord, as did David his father" (1 Kings 11:4-6).

Solomon turned away from the God Who appointed him king and blessed him above all the other kings of the world. His heart was lured by the gods of his many wives.

Now think about Judas Iscariot. What was his weakness and how did Satan play around with it? The disciples worked with Judas for three long years, but they did not know the weakness Satan would use in that disciple. However, as it always turns out, Judas' weakness was known by God, Satan, and Judas himself. The weakness is depicted in his statement as he sought an opportunity to betray the Savior in Matthew 26:15:

> "And said unto them, What will ye give me, and I will deliver
> him unto you? And they covenanted with him for thirty pieces
> of silver."

This was not the first time God revealed that Judas had a problem with money.

When Mary took very costly ointment, poured it on the feet of Jesus and wiped the Savior's feet with her hair, Judas was present. He did not receive that glorious act happily. His heart was filled with indignation. The words that proceeded from his mouth fooled those who looked on Mary with wonder, but not the Lord Jesus Christ.

"Why was not this ointment sold for three hundred pence, and given to the poor?" Judas came off as a holy and caring servant. However, Christ, Who knew Judas, gave us the true interpretation of Judas' words.

> "This he said, not that he cared for the poor; but because he was a
> thief, and had the bag, and bare what was put therein" (John 12:6).

Judas' problem was money. That is what the enemy used to tempt and to fulfill his wicked schemes. Satan was aware of Judas' problem (Luke 22:3).

What is your weakness? What will the enemy use to tempt and launch his attacks on you? What is it that can bring you down? What can you do about it? Don't think Satan will not tempt you. Temptations are a guarantee for

Christians. You must prepare. You must seal and reinforce the possible areas of invasion in your life.

It is in knowing your weaknesses that you will place specific guards in place. It is in understanding your weakness that you will live with alertness and the awareness of the most likely places the enemy will strike in your life.

Be practical in your approach. Know where you can go and where you cannot. Understand where you can be by yourself and when you must be accompanied to help you resist temptation. Know what you are most vulnerable to and seek ways to go around it. Find ways to say no. Seek an accountability partner. Share, fellowship, pray, and hold each other's hands. This is part of what it takes to resist temptations.

## 2. Think about what is at stake

Satan targets you as an individual most of the time. However, your temptation has implications for other people. The outcome of your temptation has inferences in heaven and on earth. Temptations have eternal consequences, too.

Think of the reasons why Satan tempts you. Why would the enemy work to make you fall as a married man or woman? Why would he tempt you with a man or a woman? Why would he tempt you to steal, to kill, and bear false witness?

It is because he presents you with the temptation that will have the greatest impact in your life. He goes for what will bring shame, humiliation, and embarrassment to many other people. Satan does not go for the small stuff. When the devil shows up, he wants what will blaspheme God and hinder spiritual work. He goes for the kill. That is why God warns us to be vigilant and to be sober. (1 Peter 5:8) The enemy comes only to kill, to steal and to destroy (John 10:10). When Satan tempts you, he is looking beyond you as a person.

Think about what is at stake. Why must you learn to resist temptations? What are the implications of your succumbing to temptation and falling? How will your yielding to Satan's temptations affect:

- God, God's name, and God's work?
- Your testimony?
- Your effectiveness in God's work?
- Your family?
- Your brothers and sisters?
- Those who know you?
- The generations to come?

Let this help you have a reason to resist temptation. Even in those tough hours when you are vulnerable and weak, remember that there are many people relying on your standing. Their lives will be affected in major ways should you succumb to the enemy's tricks. That is part of Satan's strategic plan for the temptation.

## Learning from the Temptations of Christ Our Savior

Let us look at the temptation of Christ and learn from it.

Christ came on earth to fulfill an eternal purpose. It was God's plan to redeem humanity right from the beginning of time. As the time ripened for God's plan, the enemy did not remain oblivious. Just as he does today, he started a wicked plan to foil the plans of God and to keep man enslaved.

In Matthew 4, our Savior was tempted. It is interesting to note that Satan embarked on his mission while Christ fasted for forty days and nights. What a time to tempt someone, let alone God. What was he thinking? Fasting heightens your spiritual senses. It helps your heart to focus on God. It helps you to desensitize and crucify your flesh while making room for the flourishing of the spirit. Fasting is a good practice for turning your focus away from worldly things to God.

Knowing that Christ was very hungry after a forty-day fast, Satan's first temptation had to do with food. "If thou be the Son of God, command that these stones be made bread," Satan said. Of course, Christ had the power to turn the rocks into bread. Satan overlooked the greater mission for which

Christ was fasting. The Savior, Who was preparing for His public ministry, was not distracted from His eternal plan.

Satan did not stop at that. He tried to make Christ tempt God. However, Christ's focus was not on momentary glory. If anything, all glory, power, and honor belonged to Him.

Lastly, Satan pulled out his dirtiest trick thinking he would make Christ yield to temptation. The devil took Christ to an exceedingly high mountain and showed the Savior all the kingdoms of the world and all their glory. Thinking he had gotten the Lord Jesus Christ, Satan said, "all these things will I give thee, if thou wilt fall down and worship me."

What a wonderful day for Satan if Christ had ascribed him majesty, glory, and honor. This sin got the devil kicked out of heaven (Isaiah 14; Ezekiel 28). He has not stopped competing with God and fighting for glory and majesty.

How could Christ succumb to such a temptation? What could make Him think about it? What made Satan think that Christ could forsake His eternal mission?

The whole earth depended on Christ (and it still does) for the cleansing and the redemption of their sins. Christ came to seek and to save all who were lost. The Savior came to reconcile man to God. Christ was focused on His mission. That was His driving force for praying, fasting, listening to God, and reaching out to those who would otherwise die in their sins. What a blessing to know that by Christ being fully God, even while He was on His earthly mission, He could not sin.

Imagine the excitement that welled up in Satan's mind as he thought of the wild possibilities resulting from the Savior's yielding to temptation. Can you fathom the celebration in Satan's mind as he thought about thwarting the plans of God?

Imagine what Satan can do to you! You are not God. You are human. Satan will bombard you with opportune temptations. He knows how easy it is to make you fall. However, you must think about your mission on earth. Why did God put you where you are? What is your role? What will the effect of your fall be? Whom will you affect by your yielding to temptation? How will it affect your family? What about your friends? What effect will it have on the church? What will it do to your testimony? What are the eternal consequences of your succumbing to temptation?

Stop and reflect on Joseph for a moment. What would have been the consequences of Joseph's yielding to his temptations? The possibilities are limitless. They could include death, castration, a lifetime in jail, never seeing of his family again, hard labor and bondage, hunger, starvation, and the absence of God's favor in his life.

## 3. Run

You will face many temptations where the most spiritual and wise thing to do is to run. It is okay to run. Regardless of your age, you must practice running. When such temptations come, don't waste time thinking and trying to reason out the circumstances. Such precarious hours can change your course quickly. If you must think, then think on your feet while running as fast as you can.

This is exactly what Joseph did. He ran.

Joseph must have seen how Potiphar's wife grabbed him and realized that the woman was serious. Remember this had gone on for days. The Bible narrates that she asked Joseph to sleep with her day after day, but he refused. She did not take Joseph's no for an answer. She sought for an opportunity to fulfill her desire. She approached Joseph as he went about his business in the house. Seeing there were no other servants in the house, she caught Joseph and gave him another direct offer to go to bed with her (Genesis 31:11-12).

It is one thing for a man or a woman to flirt. You may interpret the actions and keep yourself in safe distance. However, it is a dangerous moment for a woman to hold a man strongly desiring intimacy.

In this particular incident, it may have been easier if it were the other way round in my opinion. It feels like women have to keep their guards high to constantly say no. Nevertheless, how often do young men say no to such direct offers. I would like you to put yourself in Joseph's shoes for a moment. What would it take for Joseph to sin with Potiphar's wife? How long would it take the young man to fulfill the long-thirsted-for desire of that woman?

Literally, Joseph could have fallen by lingering on the thought. That is how most temptations begin to crack our defenses.

Had Joseph gambled with the request, his thought would have taken him on fantasy circus that pushes most Christian to sin.

Joseph could have thought on many things such as:

- Wow, I must be handsome for such an honorable woman to desire me.
- Maybe she loves me
- Maybe I will be favored and honored in this house if I do it.
- This might be a chance to walk away from slavery
- Wow! This is a rare opportunity, who gets such offers from celebrities.

Had Joseph taken time to think on such things, he would have had no chance to stand and resist. Instead of thinking, he ran.

The scheme that Potiphar's wife used still works to date. Married women still pursue young men. Young women strategically lure and seduce older men. Married men can entice women as well.

Relationships have strong pulls that can bring human beings to their knees in shame, humiliation, and regret. I have not met a man who is too strong for the seductions of a woman. No woman is powerful enough to resist the lure and sexual aggression of a man.

You may begin by resisting and praying hard against the advances of someone of the opposite gender. However, such temptations call for more than resisting and prayer. You must run away. Say no and keep the distance.

Stay away. This is because every move, touch, and request made after the first weakens you. If you don't run and stop it immediately, you will slowly begin to give in. You may start hating it, but you will be surprised to find yourself embracing, kissing, and doing more than you ever thought you would do. Have you not heard people say, "We hated one another so badly but now we are madly in love?"

Running does not apply to sexual temptations only. As you understand your weaknesses, you should know what can easily bring you down. Do not gamble with such sin. Do not stand staring at what breaks your pillars and defenses. Give yourself distance. Run. Running does not denote weakness. In fact, those who understand themselves and run out of a deliberate act of their will to avoid sin are God's most reliable men and women.

### 4. Remember, there is a way to escape

Good military generals do not plunge their armies into battle without an escape plan. Strategies of war include mapping out a plan for retreat to safety. This is because armies are not always sure of victory. Fighting involves going against deceptive schemes of your enemy. You may be good at war, but the enemy can outsmart you with lies and unpredictable maneuvers.

God, our army General, does not leave His children in battle without a way to escape either. He knows how vulnerable you are in the spiritual battle. He understands the cunningness of the enemy you fight on a daily basis. God knows the relentless power with which Satan fights you. Remember, Satan was a cherub in heaven. He was in a position of power and authority. He led heaven into music and worship.

I like the Scripture that says God looks at us and remembers we are dust (Psalm 103:14). Imagine how easy it is to trample dust underfoot. It is no wonder Christ revealed that Satan desired to sift Peter like wheat. God knows that you cannot stand against Satan on your own even if you put your best effort forward.

Whenever you face a temptation, remember to look for a door of escape. God will not allow a temptation to come your way unless He knows you can handle or that there is a clear way out to your rescue. Look at the truth of God's Words as recorded for us in 1 Corinthians 10:13:

> "There hath no temptation taken you but such as is common to man: but God is faithful, who will not suffer you to be tempted above that ye are able; but will with the temptation also make a way to escape, that ye may be able to bear it."

Think on the truth within God's message as you face temptation. It is liberating. It means you can run for safety. Imagine a bully approaching you ready for a rough fight. As you stand and look at the tall, giant-like man, your heart melts. There is no way you can dare stand and engage him in a fight. What do you do in such a case?

1. You seek reinforcement if you have a chance.
2. You throw your hands up and surrender without knowing your fate.
3. You take cover. Why stand there when you know that your best effort will only leave you with a bruised eye or a fractured skull?

The second option is not a choice for any Christian to take. You do not surrender to the devil. Satan's ultimate goal is to see you surrender and indulge in sin as you wallow in weakness.

This leaves you with the first and last option.

What does a practical approach to option one look like? How do you seek reinforcement in your time of temptation?

There are different ways to do this. Make it your habit to call on God in moments of spiritual danger. Pray. God is always only a prayer away. God promises to hear and come to your rescue in times of trouble and danger.

"Out of the depths have I cried unto thee, O LORD" (Psalm 130:1). God means it when He says, "The righteous cry, and the LORD heareth, and delivereth them out of all their troubles" (Psalm 34:17).

God is your best reinforcement. Make your call instantly. Train your heart to call on God out of a sincere and honest heart when tempted. It need not be a long prayer. In my moments of temptation, I have learned to cry out, "Lord help me."

What about your last option? How do you escape temptation? How do you do it in real life?

Understand that this is a true and real option for many spiritual battles. That door of escape is your God-given avenue to avoiding falling to temptation. For the most part, it will help you escape sin. It comes at that time of great weakness when you would have otherwise fallen. It may appear as an interruptive phone call just before you sign that bad document, yield to a deceptive kiss, lock that door, send that message or take that object. This may also be your knock at the door, the cry from your child, and the intruder. Other times, it may be the red light that delays your plans. It may be the heavy traffic. It may also be the breaking down of the car.

God's door of escape is His hand that rescues in temptations. It may be that message you get from your friend. It may be the preacher's voice from the pulpit or radio addressing your specific situation. Do not step over it and go ahead to do it. Take God's door of escape.

## Activities to Help You Make Deliberate Choices to Serve God Better

The truth is, temptations are real. Not only are temptations real but they are tough to resist. However there is even a greater truth; you resist temptations more than you think about or even give yourself credit.

1. What temptations are you facing today?
2. How can the truth of what you have learned in this chapter help you to stand and resist those temptations? What truth must you apply right now?

3.   Are there temptations in your life from which you must run? Don't play with the temptation(s). Do not go back to them. Don't look back. Don't give the devil another chance. Run.

4.   Call on God. Ask for His help with the temptation. He cares. He will come. He will help you.

5.   God always provides a way out of temptation. Look for God's door of escape. Be purposeful. Be intentional. Do not give up too soon. Be sure to find God's way of escape and get out of it.

## Memory Verse

*There hath no temptation taken you but such as is common to man:*
*but God is faithful, who will not suffer you to be tempted above that ye are*
*able; but will with the temptation also make a way to escape,*
*that ye may be able to bear it.*

1 Corinthians 10:13

# Part Four

# Stepping Out to Meet the Needs of Our Generation

## Chapter Fourteen

# Purposing to Act

*If you have men who will only come if they know there is a good road,*
*I don't want them. I want men who will come if there is no road at all.*

David Livingstone[15]

## Don't Wait for Someone Else to Act

Our generation has many diverse and complex needs. Some of the issues that surround humanity are so complex that leaders and policy makers do not have solutions to them. This is because most of the taunting issues of life have spiritual roots. Many of them will resolve only as men's hearts return to God for healing and direction. Murder, hate, crime, segregation, theft, slander, maligning, and ill treatment all stem from a degenerate heart or from a heart that is far removed from God.

Christians are God's vessels of hope for this century. I am convinced that the healing of your nation is depended on what Christians will do. The healing of your society, the institutions found therein, and even your own family or home will take place when God's children will take God at His

---

15    Livingstone, David. *Missionary Travels and Researches in South Africa.* Germany: TP Verone Publishing, 2010.

Word and act. God promises to hear, to come down, and to heal our land when we take necessary steps towards Him.

I would like us to look at a few things that Christians must do in order to display God's splendor and influence our generation in a positive way.

## 1. Return to God

God's promise is still as true for our times as it was in the days of King David and King Solomon. The apostasy that prevailed back then still prevails today. David and Solomon rose to power at a time when God's people had departed from Him. Just as it is evident in our times, everyone did what was right in their own eyes (Judges 17:6; 21:25). Truth was relative. Man did not want to be told what to do. If it felt right, he did it. If it hurt someone else, he did not care. As long as it was pleasurable and gratifying, he indulged in it, not remembering that consequences follow actions. Israel was under God's judgment.

However, God cares for His people, and He had a plan for those He loved. God's redemptive plan for the healing of His people has always been through repentance and forgiveness. God understands people—in every generation. He knows the unique challenges that people face in certain eras. He does not leave humanity desperate without hope and healing. He leaves an open door towards healing, peace, and hope. Here is God's open door even for our generation.

"If my people, which are called by my name, shall humble themselves, and pray, and seek my face, and turn from their wicked ways; then will I hear from heaven, and will forgive their sin, and will heal their land" (2 Chronicles 7:14).

It is easy to look at the tough circumstances that surround you with a passive, calloused, or indifferent heart. What is your role in what you see? Where do you step in? Let us walk together through practical steps that will affect the situations that surround us in positive ways.

You have a part to play in the healing of your nation, your society, your home, your family, and even your personal life. How do you do this?

A. Be active in identifying the role you have played
for your nation to be where it is spiritually.

Begin by taking an honest inward look. How have you contributed to the spiritual state of your church, society, and home? What have you done or failed to do that has propagated a degradation of spiritual soundness? It is easy to blame other people for the challenges and problems that surround us. It is easier to identify and to point out what leaders and other people have not done. However, God holds Christians responsible for the spiritual alertness of a home, society, and even a nation.

God charges Christians with the responsibility of praying for leaders. It is interesting to note that God links the peaceful and godly lifestyles of a nation to the prayers of His children. This is what is good and acceptable in the eyes of God.

I urge you to read this for yourself in 1 Timothy 2:1-4: "I exhort therefore, that, first of all, supplications, prayers, intercessions, and giving of thanks, be made for all men; For kings, and for all that are in authority; that we may lead a quiet and peaceable life in all godliness and honesty. For this is good and acceptable in the sight of God our Saviour; Who will have all men to be saved, and to come unto the knowledge of the truth."

As you read such a passage, it is sobering to ask yourself practical questions such as:

- How is my prayer life?
- Are my prayers regular, fervent, and powerful?
- Can my prayers turn the course of history for my nation?
- Can my prayers change the destiny of this nation?
- How much do I pray for my family members by name?
- What does God think about my prayers?
- Can God credit me as a praying Christian?
- Can God depend on me to pray for my family members, my society, and my nation?

## B. Ask God to search and reveal the true motives of your heart.

Ask God to help you see exactly for what your heart lives. When you allow the Holy Spirit to walk you through His checklist, you may marvel at the sin and rottenness that sits within you.

The Prophet Jeremiah was right when he proclaimed God's message and said that the heart of man is deceitful above all things and desperately wicked. No one can know it (Jeremiah 17:9-10).

Make it your prayer today and in the days to come to ask God to search your heart. Like David, pray, "Search me, O God, and know my heart: try me, and know my thoughts: And see if there be any wicked way in me, and lead me in the way everlasting" (Psalm 139:23-24).

As you make this prayer, take a pen and paper and be still before God. He will bring many things to your heart and mind. As long as you make this prayer from an honest heart, desiring healing and victory, God will speak. Write down everything God brings to your attention. Begin working on them one after another. Before long, you will witness healing, change, and victory.

## C. Repent on your own behalf and on the behalf of others.

I would like you to look at how a prominent man approached God in prayer when he learned that his nation was under God's hand of judgment.

Look at Daniel, a prophet and beloved man of God.

Daniel turned to God and pleaded with Him. He put on sackcloth and ashes and fasted. He repented and confessed sin to God. Look at how Daniel took on the sins of the people and the nation as his own and confessed them before God.

> "And I prayed unto the LORD my God, and made my confession, and said, O Lord, the great and dreadful God, keeping the covenant and mercy to them that love him, and to them that keep his commandments;

We have sinned, and have committed iniquity, and have done wickedly, and have rebelled, even by departing from thy precepts and from thy judgments:

Neither have we hearkened unto thy servants the prophets, which spake in thy name to our kings, our princes, and our fathers, and to all the people of the land.

O Lord, righteousness belongeth unto thee, but unto us confusion of faces, as at this day; to the men of Judah, and to the inhabitants of Jerusalem, and unto all Israel, that are near, and that are far off, through all the countries whither thou hast driven them, because of their trespass that they have trespassed against thee.

O Lord, to us belongeth confusion of face, to our kings, to our princes, and to our fathers, because we have sinned against thee.

To the Lord our God belong mercies and forgivenesses, though we have rebelled against him;

Neither have we obeyed the voice of the LORD our God, to walk in his laws, which he set before us by his servants the prophets.

Yea, all Israel have transgressed thy law, even by departing, that they might not obey thy voice; therefore the curse is poured upon us, and the oath that is written in the law of Moses the servant of God, because we have sinned against him" (Daniel 9:4-11).

Daniel was a righteous man before God. He could have been indifferent to the bad situations. After all, his heart was right with God. Daniel was diligent in his pursuit of God. Why was he to be bothered by other people's sins and plight? Moreover, he lived in the palace. Wasn't he safe? Would God's judgment get to him? After all, he did not participate in the sins of the people.

Daniel did not blame others for the collapse of the nation. It was true that he was a righteous man. It was also true that he did not participate in the sins of his people. However, Daniel saw himself right at the center of what was taking place and purposed to seek God. He repented and turned his heart to God as he cared about the future of God's people.

Daniel has a good example for those who desire to do God's work and to display His splendor. What surrounds you is not begging for your criticism. It is bad enough already. You don't have to blame those who led to it either. You don't even have to know the role each person played. Take your place at the feet of Christ and repent—for your own sins and the sins of other people.

Repentance means your heart is willing to ask God for forgiveness. It also means that you are ready to turn from wickedness back to God and do something to bring positive change. Repentance points the heart to God. True repentance means that you are ready to point other people to Christ. You are ready to see wrong as God sees it. It means you are determined to live a life that pleases God.

## 2. Take responsibility for what is happening and get involved.

If you want to change the bad situations that surround you, you must get involved. To stay away, turn a deaf ear, close your eyes, or become indifferent is to promote things of which you don't approve.

The Prophet Nehemiah faced similar situations to those that Daniel encountered. Let us look at Nehemiah's reaction when he learned that God had withdrawn His hand of protection and mercy from Israel, as recorded in Nehemiah 1.

## A. First, look at the bad news

Israel was already in exile. God allowed the Chaldeans to invade God's holy city. They captured many people, chained them, and took them to serve in a foreign land. Among them was the Prophet Nehemiah.

Few Jews escaped the raid. However, those who remained in Jerusalem faced horrifying circumstances. The Chaldeans destroyed the walls and burned down the city gates that had once protected them.

Imagine what it meant and felt like for an enemy to take away your protection and to leave you helpless and vulnerable to his attacks. The people of God lived in fear. They were under reproach.

God's children lost their coveted position. They moved from a people of honor to despised men and women. God had protected and fought for His people for years. He defeated the best armies of the world for their sake. The world feared and revered the children of Israel. Who would dare attack them? God took full responsibility for them and provided for their every need.

Nonetheless, God's children sinned and forgot the source of their abundance. God withdrew from their camps and took down their defenses. Now they had moved from abundance to poverty. From dignity, they became slaves and a laughingstock among other nations. From bravery and freedom, God's children now hid from their enemies. They lived in disgrace, humiliation, and fear.

## B. Second, look at Nehemiah's response

The prophet Nehemiah quickly identified himself with the plight of his people, weeping and mourning for days. He fasted and prayed, confessing his own sins and the sins of God's people. He prayed over injustices and crimes committed by name and repented as though he was guilty of each one of them. Then he reminded God of His promise to gather His people and to restore His name and worship among them (Nehemiah 1:5-11).

Nehemiah was one of the men who followed God wholeheartedly. He was not an evil man, nor did he participate in the sins of the land. However, he understood what it would take to see the healing of a nation.

Note that Nehemiah was in Persia when all this took place. He could have forgotten the people who remained in Jerusalem. After all, he was living in luxury. He served in the king's palace as a cupbearer. This was no small position. Nehemiah was a high-ranking officer overseeing the safety of the king within the royal courts. This was a position given to faithful and trustworthy men. He served wine to the king and maintained a confidential relationship. This high position was accorded to exceptionally few highly favored individuals in the history of humanity.

Nehemiah put his royal position to the side. He put on sackcloth and fasted in ashes.

### How Does This Relate to Us Today?

The God Who put the Prophet Nehemiah in a position of influence still does it today. God has not stopped placing His children in opportunistic positions to affect the spiritual climate of homes, societies, and nations. God created you to live in this century for the same reason. He has you in the right home, right family, and right workplace. He has planted you there to fulfill His purposes.

How are you responding to what surrounds you today?

God's ear is attentive to the prayers of His servants. In fact, He listens to the prayers of those whose walk is upright. He inclines His heart to hear the prayers of those who walk closely with Him. It is true that the fervent prayer of a righteous man prevails in times of difficulty (James 5:16).

God is waiting to hear from you. God is waiting to hear your prayers concerning the evils of our land. He wants to act on behalf of your family and society, but you must pray. Take their sins to God in repentance. Healing will not come without repentance. The wicked are not quick to repent. You must lead the way. Allow your heart to be burdened with the sins of those who surround you. This is your pathway to influencing your land.

## C. Third, look at Nehemiah's action plan (Nehemiah 2:1-8)

- Nehemiah involved the king. He purposed to let those who had the power to make things work know. He did not disguise his pain, neither did he hide it. Instead, he approached his master with a sad countenance that provoked a discussion of the issues at hand.
- Nehemiah asked the king for permission to go and rebuild the gates and walls of Jerusalem.

- Nehemiah looked at the long, treacherous, and dangerous journey and requested the king to grant him letters to the governors in whose territories he would pass to oversee his safe travel.

- Nehemiah thought through and came up with a plan to repair the damage. He presented his request to the king. He asked for plenty of wood and acquired captains of the army and horsemen to accompany him.

- Nehemiah took a journey to evaluate the damage and to establish a concrete plan on how to rebuild Jerusalem.

- Finally, Nehemiah recruited able and willing people with whom to work.

Notice that the Prophet stepped into the prevailing circumstances like everything depended on him. He did not second guess himself or wonder whether he had what was needed to do the work.

The damage in Jerusalem was extensive. The prophet could have looked on it and retreated. After all, how could one man embark on such a great task alone! Nevertheless, it did not threaten Nehemiah. I believe this was because the Sovereign Lord placed His servant in the right place. God surrounded Nehemiah with the right people and gave him the right personality and career that would help him fulfil such work.

## What about Us? How Do We Deal with Our Spiritual Damage?

We are living at a time in the history of the world when there is enormous spiritual damage in the lives of many people. Just as it was in the days of Nehemiah, our days are filled with shame and ridicule because of the destruction of the walls and gates that gave us protection and ensured our safety.

Nevertheless, God has placed us here to effect change. He surrounds us with people whose help will be instrumental in meeting the needs of our generation. God has resources to help meet the challenges of our times.

God has created you for this time. He has surrounded you with the right people and put you within the reach of many resources to meet the needs of our day. After all, the world and all its riches are from God. Those are God's resources. They are designated to meet prevailing needs regardless of which storehouse they originate.

Like the Prophet Nehemiah, ask yourself the fundamental questions that will lead to action.

- What is the need of the hour?
- What needs surround me today?
- What must I do to correct them and have victory?
- What must I do to get it done?
- How will I do it?
- What do I need?
- Whom should I ask to join in the work?

I would like to encourage you to step out and do as God nudges your heart. Take responsibility and meet the needs that surround you. Do not wait for a crew before you start. After all, most great works begin with one man or one woman before other people see its worth and join.

I like what Mother Teresa said, and the profound truth found therein as it relates to doing God's work. "I alone cannot change the world, but I can cast a stone across the water to create many ripples."

Allow your heart to be touched with the tough situations surrounding people today. Step in and be God's hands and feet. Trust God to give you what you need to fulfil the work.

Nehemiah and Ezra rebuilt the walls and the gates of the great city, Jerusalem. Today, there are many, but different, walls that are broken and in need of rebuilding. Other issues demand our action. This is your time to make positive contribution to the world around you. It is your turn. Do not lose this opportunity. Reach within your heart. Take what God has given you freely and use it to do His work in your generation. Those who change the destiny of other people's lives are men and women just like you. They hear God, trust Him, and move on to obey Him in faith knowing that God always stands with His work and with those who step out to do it.

Lift up your eyes, and look on the fields; for they are white already to harvest. (John 4:35) All you need to do is step out and you will walk into the field filled with desperate people in need of your help and the hope that only God gives.

## Activities to Help You Act Now

Allow your heart to be touched with the tough situations surrounding people today. Step in and be God's hands and feet to meet the needs. Trust God to give you what you need to fulfil the work.

1. Is God pointing at you to meet specific needs of people He is bringing your way? Identify those needs. Do not be hesitant. Follow Him and meet the needs.

2. Has your Christian walk been passive or nominal? Is your heart dull and indifferent to the pain of others? Pray. Let God restore you to Himself. Ask Him to burden your heart with the specific needs you can meet.

3. In what ways have you contributed to the current spiritual state of your family? What about the church, the community in which you live, and the nation?

4. In what ways can you make positive contributions to the spiritual and physical wellbeing of other individuals?

## Memory Verse

*For we are his workmanship, created in Christ Jesus unto good works,*
*which God hath before ordained that we should walk in them.*

Ephesians 2:10

Chapter Fifteen

# Step Up to the Times

*How wonderful it is that nobody need wait a single moment*
*before starting to improve the world.*

Anne Frank[16]

## This Is Your Chance to Do Something

God's people must step out and step up to meet the deep spiritual needs of our times. God created you with the spiritual needs of this century in mind. God wanted you to live at a time such as this in the history of the world. He has equipped you for this century and for the people you meet every day.

When wicked Haman plotted to kill the Jews around the 6th century B.C., he did not know that God had created a beautiful orphan girl to confound his plans. He did not know that for his wicked plot, God would work through ordinary and unordinary circumstances to take Esther to the royal throne as queen of Persia.

Imagine what it was like for God to dethrone the former queen in order to put an unknown young maid on the throne. This was because God created her for the times. God, Who does not create people for the mere purpose of filling up space, had work for her.

---

16   Frank, Anne. *The Diary of a Young Girl.* United Kingdom: Pan Books, 1957.

Esther's responsibility was tough. The Persian Empire was a vast dynasty, with over one hundred and twenty-seven provinces stretching across different continents, including Persia, (now Iran) India, and parts of Egypt.

Persia had the most powerful army in the world. Every nation on the face of the earth feared them. Kings feared and reverenced this powerful and merciless nation. If you heard they were headed your way, you had to surrender and seek peace at all cost. No army dared to fight against Persia.

The man whom Esther married was pompous, royal, powerful, and likened to a god. When King Ahasuerus stood to speak, the whole world listened. When he displayed his riches and the glories of his royal majesty, it was breathtaking and something to stop and behold. His wealth was enormous. We are talking of a man who would throw a luxurious party to thousands of dignitaries and common people for six straight months. Every man was treated to what he desired. The vessels used were not ordinary either. They were made of gold and different one from another.

God is sovereign, but He also has a sense of humor. He is a mastermind of plans. It was to such royalty and fame that He elevated an orphan girl. Mordecai, who took Esther for his own daughter following the death of her parents, was a captive. Mordecai was one of the Jews whom King Nebuchadnezzar captured in Jerusalem and carried into Babylon. Now imagine that the heart that beat for the purposes of God in Esther was created and nurtured for such elevated excellent opportunity. (Read Esther 1 and 2 to understand the whole narrative.)

Mordecai, who understood the times in which he lived, appealed to Esther's heart when he learned that Haman was plotting to kill the Jews. This seasoned man of God rose to the times for which he was created. Mordecai tore his clothes, put on sack clothes with ashes, and went into the city and cried aloud. He marshalled the Jews and there was great weeping and wailing as the Lord's people sought God in fasting and sack clothes (Esther 4:1-4).

Mordecai did not stay in the trenches where his voice could not be heard nor where his influence could not be felt. He went to the king's gates, right there in the palace, with his sack clothes and ashes. He carried with him the letters decreeing the killing and annihilation of the Jews. He even disclosed the amount of money Haman promised to pay in order to see God's people destroyed. Mordecai was not afraid to reveal the wicked schemes of Haman, a high-ranking official who worked in the palace and advised the king.

Mordecai also understood the position to which God had raised Esther. Look at the message he sent Queen Esther in Esther 4:13-14:

> "Think not with thyself that thou shalt escape in the king's house, more than all the Jews. For if thou altogether holdest thy peace at this time, then shall there enlargement and deliverance arise to the Jews from another place; but thou and thy father's house shall be destroyed: and who knoweth whether thou art come to the kingdom for such a time as this?"

## The Implication of Mordecai's Message to Esther for Our Times
What is the implication of Mordecai's message to Esther in our time?

### 1: Let the needs that surround you affect your heart.

Mordecai's first message to Esther reminded her of who she was: a Jew. Regardless of her royalty and fame, she was a Jew. Mordecai's message essentially said, "Wake up, my little girl. These are your people. If they die, you will, too. You are sheltered from their plight right now, but you cannot forget them." What a reminder for God's children today. What affects God's children must be your concern. We are of the same body. When one member suffers, we all suffer with them; if one member is honored, all members rejoice (1 Corinthians 12:26).

This means that God expects you to be mindful of what other Christians are facing. Your heart cannot be indifferent. You cannot live in your little haven and enjoy life while turning a blind eye to the plight of God's children.

God is asking us the same question He asked Zerubbabel in Haggai 1:4. At a time when God's house remained in ruins there were people who did not care as long as they were comfortable in their own homes. As long as they were not affected by the attack that took place under King Darius when He destroyed Israel, they were fine.

"Is it time for you, O ye, to dwell in your cieled houses, and this house lie waste?"

For our time, God may still be asking the same question. "Why are you so comfortable in your own house while my house remains in ruins? Why is your heart indifferent and unaffected with what is happening in God's place of worship?"

Other issues are of concern in this age, too. Those who will stand and display God's splendor in our times must allow their hearts to be touched by what surrounds them. Many who are oppressed by Satan are your brothers and sisters. Those who have lost their mind, their peace, and even hope can be found in the house of God. Think about those addicted to various things—elicit substances, medications, pornography, sex, money, food, and disturbing behaviors. Those imprisoned by their choices are seeking help. The poor, destitute, forsaken, and marginalized are depending on those who are able to help them.

What do you have? What is your position? What influence can you bring to the situations that surround you?

2: Look at what is happening around you with a spiritual eye.

Look at the second part of Mordecai's message to Esther stated in Esther 4:14:

"For if thou altogether holdest thy peace at this time, then shall there enlargement and deliverance arise to the Jews from another place; but thou and thy father's house shall be destroyed."

What is Mordecai telling the young queen?

He is appealing to what is obvious and already known about Esther.

In essence, Mordecai is telling her, "I am sitting at the gates of your palace because I believe the deliverance of God's people lies in your hands. You are in a position to act. You have power to do something. Your words and actions are important. God has given you what we need. You are God's channel of hope, mercy, and deliverance. The many Jews whose cries fill the towns and the cities are echoing your name. However, the choice is in your hands. You can arise and do something, or you can hide in the majestic royal palace and act as if you do not know them. Nevertheless, remember, should you choose the latter, God will still find help for His people, but you and your father's house shall be destroyed."

As you read this, there are people who are looking to you for help. They know you. They know your standing with God. God has put you in their path for a reason. They are awaiting God's hand of mercy to act through you. They covet your help.

You must understand a few things as you make up your mind on what to do.

Do not take everything at face value. Look beyond the person and focus on the spiritual need. Some inner spiritual needs are smudged and camouflaged by the outward appearances or physical needs. It is by getting to the physical needs and by looking beyond their physical displays that you will minister to the individual.

Understand, too, that God does not force you to act. Like Esther, you have a choice. This is your time. You can act if you want, or you can be cold, intolerant, and indifferent. Remember that God cares for His people and He will not leave them desolate. He will raise people who will get in the trenches to work and use strangers who are unknown to them. It is a privilege for you to serve and help God's people.

### 3: This is your time to act.

Mordecai's message to Esther still applies to us today. Your heart will not enjoy hearing these words every day. This is because of the truth they carry. They remind us of our nothingness apart from the grace of God.

Mordecai's words were sobering. "And who knoweth whether thou art come to the kingdom for such a time as this?" (Esther 4:14).

It is hard not to imagine what was going on in the older man's mind as he sent the message to the young woman he raised. You can almost hear Mordecai saying, "Look here, Hadassah! (Esther's Hebrew name) You know how I raised you. You were not born in a palace. Nothing could have given you that place of honor and influence had it not been for the great God, Yahweh. You did not work for this position. You did not labor day and night to be where you are. God gave it to you. God did it because He saw the future of His people. It is for this specific moment that God raised you. It is for this time that He made you beautiful. It was because of His people that God caused Queen Vashti to disobey her husband so she would be dethroned. It is for this specific time that God has been working behind the scenes in your life. Now, go and act on behalf of God and His people. Who knows that you have come to the kingdom at such a time as this in the history of God's people?"

Can you identify with Esther? Do you have God's favor in your life? Has God taken you from the ashes of the world to a place of honor? Are you enjoying the blessings of God?

How is your influence among the people of God? Are you seeking God and looking at those who surround you with a spiritual eye?

It is easy to be comfortable in your lovely surroundings without remembering the cry and the needs of those around you. It is easy to take things for granted. You may even get to a point where your heart is annoyed by the needs of God's children.

Remember, they have a right to seek your help. You are God's help to them. They see you for what God has done. God has filled you with His treasure for them. Would you prefer to be God's channel of blessings to them or to be in their shoes?

Make yourself available to God. Have the mindset of a valuable and useful servant. Do not belittle or despise yourself. Do not downplay what God has put in your hand for His work either.

God uses ordinary people to bring about great changes. He uses common men and women to affect the lives of His people. Those who give hope and point man to the all-sufficient Savior are brethren whose hearts listen to God and beat with a desire to do what He says.

You don't have to be a "somebody" to do God's work and bring change in the world today. Your profile does not have to stand out. You don't have to make the pages of the internet and magazines or newspapers. As a matter of fact, no one but God needs to know you. God uses anybody. Those who are available and obedient experience the working of God through their lives.

God's formula in 1 Corinthians 1:27-29 is still powerful and effective. "But God hath chosen the foolish things of the world to confound the wise; and God hath chosen the weak things of the world to confound the things which are mighty; And base things of the world, and things which are despised, hath God chosen, yea, and things which are not, to bring to nought things that are: That no flesh should glory in his presence."

## What about You?

Esther and Mordecai were in the king's courts at an opportune time to foil the wicked schemes of Haman against God's people. What about you? Where has God put you in this season? What is your role? What needs surround you today?

The Psalmist lifted his heart to God in Psalm 123:2-3 saying, "Behold, as the eyes of servants look unto the hand of their masters, and as the eyes of a maiden unto the hand of her mistress; so our eyes wait upon the LORD our God, until that he have mercy upon us. Have mercy upon us, O LORD, have mercy upon us: for we are exceedingly filled with contempt."

I wonder how many people look to God in desperation as they wait for you to act. How are you using your position today? What about your God-given favor? What can your work, ministry, group, or organization do to display God's splendor and to bring hope to others?

God raised Joseph and sent him to Egypt to preserve many lives from a deadly famine. His circumstances were not favorable. However, Joseph looked at the events with a spiritual eye. He followed God wholeheartedly and lived to fulfil the purposes for which God created him (Genesis 45).

The Prophet Elijah rebuilt the broken alters in Israel and re-established worship among God's people. He stood against the false teachings of the times and challenged the prophets of Baal. He stood for God's truth (1 Kings 18). What about you?

Paul contended for the faith. He arose in his time as a student of the Bible, a scholar who defended the gospel of truth. He taught and trained many in the way of righteousness. He left everything and followed Christ wholeheartedly (Philippians 3).

Solomon built a house of worship to God and established protocols of worship for God's people.

God raised Gideon to deal with the shame and humiliation that prevailed among God's people. Gideon did not know that he was a mighty man in the eyes of God. Little did he understand the treasures of God within him. He stood against the Midianites and put an end to their constant wars, which sent God's people out of their homes to live in caves, mountains, and strongholds.

The midwives who feared God in Egypt saved the male children. Despite Pharaoh's decree to kill every male child, they preserved the genealogy of Israel. God blessed the midwives and gave them families of their own (Exodus 1).

## What about you?

Can you rebuild what is destroyed in the temples of worship today? Can you rebuild walls, restore prayer and the reading of God's Word like Ezra?

Can you restore true worship and tear down the shows and performances that leave God's people empty and hopeless without spiritual foundations?

Can you guide man back to the all-sufficient Savior Who can heal, deliver, clean, and meet all his needs? Will you work and stand to restore meaning and purpose in the lives of those who are bound?

In Christ, those possessed with devils are set free.

In Christ, the lunatic is restored to his right mind.

In Christ, all who are sick with different maladies get healed.

Those who are spiritually blind regain their sight and behold the Savior. The spiritually blind, the confused, and those without direction, are restored. Above all, the soul that is sick from sin—the greatest plague to the soul of man—is forgiven, washed, cleansed, set free, and made whole.

Can you be an Esther, Gideon, Samson, Mordecai, Peter, Elijah, or the midwife who fears God? Why are you where you are at a time such as this?

## Activities to Help You Step up to the Times

God created you with the spiritual needs of this century in mind. God wanted you to live at a time such as this in the history of the world. God has equipped you for this century and for the people you meet every day.

1. How can you rebuild what is destroyed in the temples of worship today? How can you rebuild spiritual foundational

walls? How can you restore prayer and the reading of God's Word like Ezra?

2.    How can you restore true worship? Can you tear down shows and performances that leave God's people empty and hopeless without spiritual foundations?

3.    How can you guide man back to the all-sufficient Savior Who can heal, deliver, clean, and meet all his needs?

4.    How can you work and stand to restore meaning and purpose in the lives of those who are bound?

## Memory Verses

*Is it time for you, O ye, to dwell in your cieled houses, and this house lie waste?*

*Go up to the mountain, and bring wood, and build the house; and I will take pleasure in it, and I will be glorified, saith the LORD.*

Haggai 1:4, 8

Chapter Sixteen

# Say Yes and Watch God Work

*Not all of us can do great things. But we can do small things with great love.*

Mother Teresa[17]

## God Is Calling on You to Work Today

Have you received an offer to which you said no but later wished you had said yes?

I heard of a company that approached a man to build a booster tower on a tiny section of his land. The man declined without listening to the rest of the conversation. The company went to the neighbor and struck a deal. Later, the man learned that his neighbor earned about $1,800 per month from the project that covered only a few feet of his property.

Every Christian has an offer from God to work in His vineyard and to display His splendor and power. God presents these offers on a daily basis. Unfortunately, it is easy to reject them. Many Christians miss them.

God's offers are wonderful. However, His work calls for commitment. It takes time. Many times, it looks worthless and unprofitable. This is because

---

17   Benenate, Becky., *Teresa, Mother. No Greater Love.* United States: New World Library, 1997.

God is not always in the business of instant gratification. God does His work thoroughly. He looks at everything from an eternal point of view. He shapes, grooms, and molds you to produce fruit that abides till the end of time to be credited to your account. His work takes time before you see fruit—the obvious outward signs.

You must engage your eye of faith and appreciate how wonderful God's offers are. If you are a Christian who enjoys praise and a boosted ego, it is easy to say no to God's offer. This is because you will find it boring, wasting time, and yielding very little.

For the Christian who likes respect, honor, and self-worth, God's offer may look ridiculous and even foolish, to say the least. This is because, to the world, God's work does not make sense. When looked at in terms of economic and financial gains, the world scoffs at it. It looks as if you must labor without pay or positive returns. This is true only for the Christian who has never engaged or immersed himself in God's work with an honest and sincere heart. I know for sure that you cannot charge God with neglect when it comes to His children. In fact, I have never met anyone who pays better than God. God's pay is different from what the secular world pays, but He is good at what He does.

## God Uses the Ordinary

God uses ordinary people to do His work. This can be disturbing to many people, including Christians. The world in which we live demands that you must be "a somebody" before you can do something. You must go to school in order to get a good job. You must possess a degree before you can belong to a particular crowd. You must prove yourself before you can be promoted and entrusted with certain responsibilities.

God's assignments do not always follow this order. God begins with anybody. He works with the skilled and the amateur alike. As long as you are willing and available, there is no limit to what God will help you do. Once you say yes, He does not plunge you into the work and watch you sink or swim. He equips you and makes sure you have all you need to do a good job. As you stick with Him, He entrusts you with different assignments as you grow, gain skills, and become a reliable worker.

God uses unlikely people to do His work and to accomplish mighty things in the world. I am sure you have heard it said that the ground is level at the foot of the cross. You can interpret this in different ways to include working for God. Paul, while speaking to the Church in Corinth reminded them of this great fact.

It is fascinating and consoling to know that:
- God did not choose the wise (by human standards).
- God did not choose the noble and influential.
- God did not choose the mighty and powerful.
- God did not choose the wealthy and those who were able.

Instead, look at the crowd that God called to accomplish His work.
- God chose the foolish things in order to shame the wisdom of the world.
- God chose the weak things of the world.
- God chose those despised by the world.
- God chose the lowly and rejected things.
- God chose what was useless, valueless, and unprofitable.

God revealed the reason for His choices in the same passage in 1 Corinthians 1:26-31. This is a safeguard for His children against self-destruction. Can you imagine the arrogance with which man would work for God thinking he was good, smart, competent, and indispensable? Can you imagine how much we would look down at each other in the same vineyard?

God did it so that no flesh could glory in His presence. This puts all of us on the same level before Him. We are chosen by Him, groomed and equipped to do His work. Our own hearts condemn us reminding us of what we were before we were greatly helped by God. When we boast, we all appreciate what He did and how He helped us. We boast in Him alone.

In fact, look around and see the numerous people God picked from the gutters of life to serve Him. Look at the amazing works God has accomplished and is still doing in their lives. We all like Newton, the slave trader, can see the grace of God that transforms wrecks, cleans their lives, and sets their feet on noble and honorable ground to serve the Living God with dignity and honor.

## You Are a Candidate

You are a candidate for God's use. God uses people like you to accomplish great works. In fact, people like you is all God has in His hands for use. They are ordinary people who display His splendor as they work wholeheartedly with their eyes on God's eternal reward.

Look at Moses, the man chosen to lead millions of people from Egypt to the land of promise.

- Moses was under a death sentence before he even entered the world. The nobles of the land did not care for him. He was not wanted (Exodus 1-2).

- His parents, Amram and Jochebed, were slaves (Exodus 6:20). They had no rights of their own. They were under heavy bondage with nothing to call their own in the world. How much does a slave possess or own? Under what class would you classify him in the economic rankings of the world?

- After birth, Moses was a wanted child. Pharaoh wanted all male children killed. Moses' parents had no choice but to hide the baby. How long can you hide a baby before he reveals himself without asking? How do you suppress his cries? How did his parents do it for the hours they had to work in the scorching sun as slaves?

- Humanly speaking, Moses had few chances of survival as a child. Just as your Sunday school told it, his parents made a little basket (ark) from reeds. They dabbed it with tar, put the baby therein, and floated it on the River Nile to flee from Pharaoh's soldiers who would have killed the child.

- It took God to protect the baby. Obviously, this is because He had a purpose for Moses. Otherwise, it looks like a ridiculous thing to do and a cruel way to end the life of the child. How would they keep off the large reptiles for which the Nile was known? What would the baby eat? What would prevent him from drowning? How long would the child survive? What if no one picked him, what would be the last thing to lead to his death?

- Moses was rescued. He lived in Pharaoh's palace for the first forty years of his life. However, like any of us, Moses made mistakes that kicked him out of what looked like a path to success. He killed a Hebrew. When the act was known, he ran for his life with nothing but a shepherd's staff in his hand. From what looked like the pinnacle of a man's life, Moses found himself with nothing in his hands. Just as he was in the River Nile in that little basket, there he was again, alone, vulnerable, homeless, and at the mercy of other people. Have you been here?

- Despite the training, the pampering, and the good education he received, Moses still had significant limitations. He stammered and was not eloquent in speech. In fact, Moses told God that he had never been good at speaking and things had not changed (Exodus 4:10).

  I would like you to take a moment to think about what Moses is implying here. "Lord, I was born with a disability. My childhood did not help it. I know you gave me an opportunity in Pharaoh's courts where I had access to the best resources but those did not help either. My past circumstances have been tough and beyond explaining. I think they added to my troubles. They made my situation worse. Lord, this is just who I am. I am not the kind of person you can use." Can you find a phrase with which to identify here?

- God asked Moses to go back to Egypt. How can you go back to the scene of your crime without causing or experiencing serious problems? Serving God is not always easy! I do not know about you, but He does not let His children get away with their mistakes. However long it may take, His clock may click slowly, but He always gets back to your heart.

- How was Moses going to face the very people from whom he fled? You talk about stammering! Moses was about to know what real stammering looked like. It is one thing to think about it in your own mind or to see it on a non-consequential scale but is another thing to see it live while standing before the honorable dignitaries of renown lands and kingdoms.

- Don't you find yourself feeling bad for Moses even though he is dead and all that is passed away?

- How do you face the most fierce and well-known army in the world at the time with a shepherd's staff in your hand? Doesn't the world have a reason to scoff, laugh, and mock at the Christian in such times?

- That is why I noted in the earlier chapters that sometimes serving God may look embarrassing and ridiculous.

However, when all is said and done, these are the people whom God uses. It is in taking us back to the messes of our lives that we genuinely turn from them in repentance unto Him. It is in confronting us with our weaknesses and vulnerabilities that we see our insufficiency and the need for God. It is in those moments that He takes away the filthy rags and replaces them with garments dipped in His precious blood. Righteous garments that cover our nakedness, our awkwardness, and our shame. It is here that He endows us with His strength and power. When we arise from His presence, we have nothing of our own on which to lean or boast but His strength made perfect in our weaknesses, and His power filling our reins ready to do His bidding.

Yes, you are a candidate. Is God taking you back to what you do not desire to remember? Has He unearthed what you thought was safely and securely buried in your sea of forgetfulness? Are you faced with embarrassing situations? Are you feeling humiliated and ashamed? Do not run away. This is your time of healing. Like a wound that has gone septic, allow God to remove the fake scabs that are covering it while on the inside it is gangrenous and oozy. Cooperate and let God lead you to true healing. Do as He instructs. And ask for forgiveness from everyone He brings to your attention.

Do not be afraid. It shall be well. He is interested in you. You are His candidate. It is your turn. He will heal your stinging wound. He will pour in His healing balm. The Holy Spirit will nurse, sooth, refresh, and bring peace, joy, and hope.

## Activities to Help You Say Yes and Watch God Work

God takes us back to the messes of our lives that we may genuinely turn from them in repentance unto Him. It is in confronting us with our weaknesses and vulnerabilities that we see our insufficiency and the need for God. This is how He molds servants for His noble use.

1. Do you have an offer for service from God? To what is He calling you?

2. Does God's offer look small, unfulfilling, and lacking in prestige?

3.  Do you classify yourself among the "nothings" whom God cannot use? Don't be afraid. You are just a vessel. Say yes and let God work through you.

4.  Is God reconciling you to Himself? Is he pointing back to past mistakes in your life? Don't be dismayed. Get back to Him. Deal with each issue accordingly. God is interested in your cleansing. You are a vessel for His use today. However, you must be clean.

## Memory Verses

*But in a great house there are not only vessels of gold and of silver, but also of wood and of earth; and some to honour, and some to dishonour.*

*If a man therefore purge himself from these, he shall be a vessel unto honour, sanctified, and meet for the master's use, and prepared unto every good work.*

2 Timothy 2:20-21

*Chapter Seventeen*

# God Is at Work in Your Life

*Don't worry about failures, worry about the chances you miss*
*when you don't even try.*

Jack Canfield[18]

## God Is at Work Behind the Scenes

I would like you to look back at God's hand in Moses' life from birth until that moment. There was not a single moment God was not involved in his life.

- It was God Who designed Moses in his mother's womb. He created him with all the intricate attributes necessary for His work. His speech impediment was part of those needful qualities.

- God chose the parents to whom Moses was born. He could have allowed Moses to be born to Pharaoh but He didn't.

- God dictated the time of Moses' birth. He could have planned for Moses to be born before or after the Pharaoh's reign but He didn't.

- God was there to protect Moses before his parents thrust him in the River Nile. Pharaoh's army was vigilant and thorough.

---

18    Canfield, Jack., Hansen, Mark Victor. *Chicken Soup for the Parent's Soul: Stories of Love, Laughter and the Rewards of Parenting.* United States: Chicken Soup for the Soul, 2012.

Nothing could have hindered them from finding and killing baby Moses.

- God was there to protect the basket in which Moses was hid. It had to take God to keep such fresh, juicy, tender, innocent, and helpless prey from the alligators of the Nile.

- God was there to guide baby Moses to the maids who took him to Pharaoh's courts. To how many possible and different directions could the basket drift? How many other people if not things would have found the baby in the Nile River?

- God was there to protect the baby from Pharaoh's verdict even after he was taken to the palace. Who keeps his enemy to feed, nurture, educate, and train?

- God stood with Moses even in the time of his troubles. The Hebrew were slave drivers. They were skilled at the job. What was one man to them had they wanted to avenge for the man Moses killed?

- God was with Moses as he traversed the long dreadful wilderness. He protected him from harm. Moses could have lost his life, and no one would have known had it not been for God. Only the animals could have known and celebrated as they enjoyed every bite.

- God was there to lead Moses to Jethro's house in Midian. In tenderness, and grace, God led His chosen man to the house of a priest. Do not underrate what that must have meant and done for Moses—a lonely and forsaken man—who had lost everything.

## God's Power Will Groom and Transform You

What a transformative work God did in the life of Moses. God walked with him as He worked in his life. Moses became a leader in ways he must never have imagined. God made an army general out of the wimp that Moses saw in himself. God turned the despondent man into a prophet incomparable to any that lived in Israel.

This is the same God Who took an unknown little shepherd boy, trained him, and made a mighty warrior who killed Goliath. He took David from the wilderness and from the sheepcote, from following sheep to be ruler and governor over Israel. God did not use the orators of the day, or the wise men of the times to write the magnificent Psalms we read and enjoy today. It was the unknown son of Jesse—chosen and groomed by God—that did it (2 Samuel 7:8).

God does not disqualify you from those who will display His splendor in our times. Before you think differently, look at the man God chose to build the magnificent place of worship in Israel. Look at the young man who led God's people to sacrifice and to worship until the glory of God filled the temple unlike anything many had seen before. It was Solomon of David—yes born of Bathsheba, the wife of Uriah, whom David took to wife. Solomon had every reason to think he did not belong. He could have taken himself outside the bracket of God's great vessels of his time.

God's eyes do not see what man sees. God is eternal and sovereign. He knows you more than you know yourself. It is God Who created you for these times. He knows the treasures He has put in you for His use and glory.

Who would have dreamed that the gospel could get to Syria through a little slave girl. Remember, Syria, the nation with the greatest army of its time! God did not use the mighty or the forceful to get to the heart of Syria. God got in by first touching Naaman, a chief officer and army commander who was also a leper. It was the firm testimony of an adolescent girl about God that paved way for the gospel to get to a pagan land. It was the unshakable faith and belief in God that could not be thwarted amidst tough and bitter circumstances that displayed God's splendor. At a time when the little girl should have cried her heart out, she was thinking of God. At a time when she would have justified her emotions to curse, resent, and be rude to her captors, she recommended God to her enemy.

I do not want to underrate the bitter situations life throws to God's children every day. However, we have God Who stands on our side. He fights for us. He does not allow anything to come to us without allowing it. Not only does God allow it but He also weighs it and permits only what you can handle. You can display His splendor and glory amidst what He allows to come your way.

## This Is Your God

What methods would you employ if you had an important message to pass to the whole world? If you were to choose twelve people, companies, or agencies to help you, whom would you include on your list?

Let me take a guess at what your list would look like in this century.

| | | |
|---|---|---|
| CEO Walmart<br>CEO Facebook<br>CEO Google<br>CEO Apple | YouTube<br>WhatsApp<br>CEO Nike<br>CEO Microsoft | CEO Alphabet<br>CEO Amazon<br>CEO Toyota<br>CEO Samsung |

How did I do?

Whom do you have on your list?

Am I close?

From my hypothetical choices, it will be a common answer to pick the most influential people and their corporations. Your choices will include people or companies who will get the job done. That is why you will choose those whose past performances speak for themselves. In this time and age, I am sure you will be looking at the most efficient and fastest way to get your information to the world. You will select what will appeal to the world and what will have the greatest impact. I doubt that the owner of your local retail store made your list. I am curious to know if your pastor is on that list, too. I wonder what came to your mind first when you embarked on the challenge.

Now, I would like you to put yourself in the feet of Christ for a moment. I know that sounds insane, but I promise you my head is still on my shoulders!

Whom would you choose to spread the gospel in the world? I really don't think anyone on Christ's list would have been on ours. I mean, how do you take fishermen—men who talked to fish and interacted with water all of their time? What skills or education did they have to merit the Savior's list? How long would it take to train those whose minds were dull to academic rigor?

Oh! But look at what God did for them and through them. How many in our days belong to that circle of witnessing 3,000 souls come to the Savior in a single meeting? Even the disciples themselves were perplexed and shocked at what proceeded from them. I believe it was with such awe and wonder that Luke wrote saying, "Now when they saw the boldness of Peter and John, and perceived that they were unlearned and ignorant men, they marvelled; and they took knowledge of them, that they had been with Jesus" (Acts 4:13).

## What about Today?

Who but God could transform a shoemaker like William Carey into a pioneer missionary to make way for the gospel in dark times?

Who but God could transform a man like D. L. Moody from a shoe salesperson to an impactful preacher in different continents?

Who but God could take David Livingstone from the environment of affluence of life to give him a tender and loving heart for the little smoke-filled huts of Africa and to open the Dark Continent to the gospel?

I am sure you know men and women whom God has saved, cleaned up, and used to accomplish His mighty works in your time.

Today, we live in dark times. The heart of man is calloused. There is an increasing indifference towards God. There is an outward rebellion and a sniffing toward Him. This is not different from other centuries. Remember pioneers of faith lived in ages when man was an idol worshipper. Just as men and women believed, stepped out, and stood for God, here is our opportunity.

The heart of man is empty. The aching of the inner soul leaves him sleepless and restless. A life devoid of God is capable of anything. That is why men and women are looking for satisfaction in entertainment, addictions, associations, adventures, and indulgences among other things.

Many who seem very angry and find destructive ways to release it are empty and needy at heart. The desperation of man's heart drives him to experiment with dangerous and harmful situations and substances. The quest will only increase and so will the danger. The outcomes will be disastrous. However, God has put you here for a purpose. It is with the challenges of our society and generation at heart that God created you and allowed you to live and to be where you are at a time such as this.

You are God's candidate. You are God's choice for this generation. Think of your unlikely journey with God. Think of the places He has stood with you even while you were far and estranged from Him. Remember His protection, His tender care, mercy, and compassion. God has been watching over you. He has been guiding your steps to Himself. This is because He has been grooming you for the times. Will you say yes and display His splendor?

## Activities to Help You Work with God in This Generation

God's eyes do not see as man's eyes. God is eternal and sovereign. He knows you more than you know yourself. It is God Who created you for the times. He knows the treasures He has put in you for His use and glory.

1. On what kind of a journey has God taken you since you surrendered your life to Him?

2. In what ways has God's hand of power worked in your life to bring you to where you are today?

3. In what ways is God grooming you for His work?

4. In what ways are you disqualifying yourself from God's service today?

5. Bow before God and ask Him what He wants you to do:
   - Today
   - In this nation
   - For this generation
   - For future generations

God does not disqualify you from those who will display His splendor in our times. He has fashioned you for today. He is molding you for the times.

## Memory Verse

*Ye have not chosen me, but I have chosen you, and ordained you,*
*that ye should go and bring forth fruit, and that your fruit should remain:*
*that whatsoever ye shall ask of the Father in my name, he may give it you.*

John 15:16

# Do Not Hoard the Bread

How has this book helped you? Have you benefited from its content? Do not hoard this spiritual bread from others who need it.

- Share what you have learned in this book with others.
- Start a Bible study or a prayer or accountability group to study the contents of this book together.
- Use it in your Sunday school class.
- Take this content and use it as a stepping-stone to bring positive influence in other people's lives.

For more information about
## Amilliah Kenya
and
## *For the Display of His Splendor*
please visit:

www.amilliahkenya.org

For more information about
AMBASSADOR INTERNATIONAL
please visit:

www.ambassador-international.com

## More from Amilliah Kenya

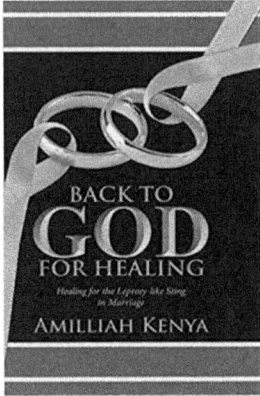

BACK TO **GOD** FOR HEALING
*Healing for the Leprosy like Sting in Marriage*
AMILLIAH KENYA

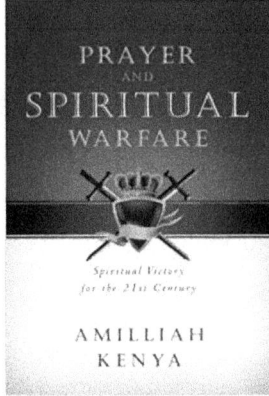

PRAYER AND **SPIRITUAL** WARFARE
*Spiritual Victory for the 21st Century*
AMILLIAH KENYA

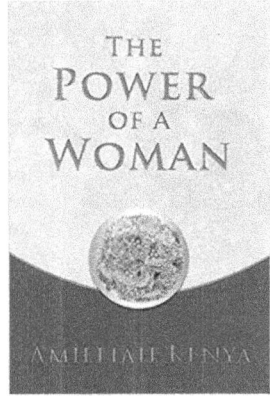

THE **POWER** OF A **WOMAN**
AMILLIAH KENYA

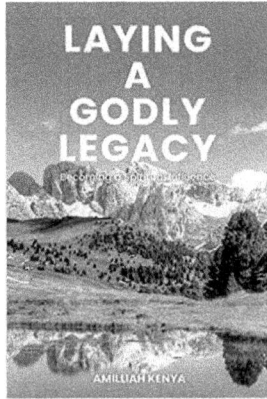

LAYING A **GODLY** LEGACY
AMILLIAH KENYA

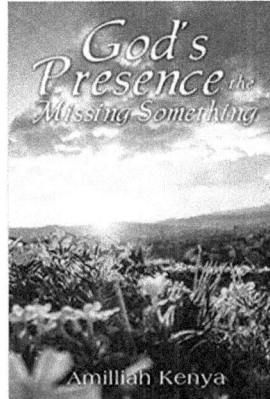

God's **Presence** the Missing Something
Amilliah Kenya

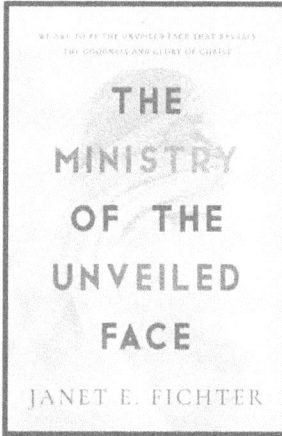

*The Ministry of the Unveiled Face* grounds us in the simplicity of sharing Christ in the everyday. The meekness of the call lies in our being responsive and obedient to God's prompting as we interact with others. Anchored in persevering prayer, we speak scriptural truths into the lives of others as the Holy Spirit leads. Like the unveiling of a beautiful bride at her wedding, the spiritual veil is removed and Christ's truth and goodness are revealed.

As we walk through dark times in our lives, we all need a way of Finding Truth in the Tempest. Faythelma Bechtel knows the tempest, but she also knows the One Who calms the storm. After losing two daughters and her husband, Faythelma has clung tighter to her Savior and longs to help others who are struggling to find peace in their own storms. This devotional journal is not meant to be read as a daily plan, but instead offers meditations on Scripture to help for your unique circumstance.

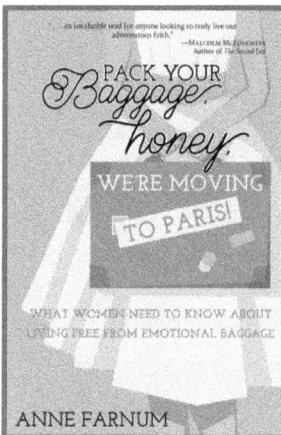

We all have something that keeps us from living fully for the Lord, but Christ wants us to give our baggage to Him so we can follow Him freely. In *Pack Your Baggage, Honey, We're Moving to Paris!* Anne Farnum explores the different kinds of baggage we carry. She also focuses on the baggage that King Saul hid behind and compares it to that which David left behind to run toward the giant.

www.ingramcontent.com/pod-product-compliance
Lightning Source LLC
Chambersburg PA
CBHW071435090426
42737CB00011B/1672